# 100% DEDUCTIBLE

*Tax-Advantaged
Pension & Retirement Plans
for Small Business*

# D. Kirk Buchanan

# 100% DEDUCTIBLE
## Tax-Advantaged Pension & Retirement Plans for Small Business

Publisher: International Legal Publishing Co.
Editor: Lon L. Davis
Cover Design: Renderings, Inc.
Typeface: Times New Roman 11/13
Press: Cameron Belt

ISBN: 0-9654078-3-7

PRINTED IN THE UNITED STATES OF AMERICA

0  9  8  7  6  5  4  3  2  1

# 100%
# DEDUCTIBLE

*Tax-Advantaged*
*Pension & Retirement Plans*
*for Small Business*

Also by D. Kirk Buchanan:


**Understanding IRAs**
*An Amiable Approach*


**The IRA Explanation**
*A User's Guide
to the
Individual Retirement Account*


*This publication is available at special prices for groups
or organizations purchasing large quantities.
For information address:
International Legal Publishing Company
P. O. Box 2041
Forney, Texas 75126*

*To Kimber,*
*Karington, Kaden, and Kauland*

# PREFACE

While the definition of "small business" is debatable, many would agree with the classification of businesses with 500 or fewer employees as such. Arguably, those businesses with between 500 and 5,000 employees might be considered mid-sized businesses. And those with over 5,000 employees, without a doubt, are large businesses. The tax-advantaged plans described in this book can be used by any size business, whether small, medium, or large. This book was written, however, with the specific needs in mind of the small business owner or executive.

Of the roughly 1.8 million independent companies with between 5 and 99 employees, only about 10% are currently benefiting from a tax-deferred savings plan, such as a 401(k) plan. Of those 1.8 million companies with between 5 and 99 employees, approximately 75% of those actually have fewer than 20 employees, according to Cerulli Associates, a Boston based research firm.

The purpose of this book is to provide executives and owners of small businesses an introductory explanation of the general types of retirement funding vehicles available to them on a tax advantaged basis. As with my previous books, I have tried to provide a non-technical approach to a very technical subject. I have tried to keep each chapter short and simple in order to provide a basic understanding without being confusing. Some of the rules may still seem technical, but as I always say, "that's because they are." Use the knowledge gained from this book to ask questions.

With the constant changes in tax laws, those of us involved with tax-qualified retirement plans are continually faced with new and complicated rules to follow. I can not express enough the importance of both a tax adviser in determining the type of plan that's right for a particular business, and an investment consultant for assistance in choosing the proper investments for the plan and the allocation of those investments within the plan. I know that sounds like the standard caveat, but never underestimate the importance of these professionals. The tax code is too complex to take lightly. As such, retirement planning is a complicated endeavor and you will need more help than one book can provide.

Some of the information in this book may be useful to the retirement planning professional as a handbook for use in daily operations. For the most part, however, it is written for the person who simply wants to get an explanation of what types of tax-advantaged plans are available and the basic differences between them.

Much of the technical information can be researched further by reading the IRS Publication 560. This can be obtained from most local IRS offices or by calling the toll free IRS Forms and Publications Center at 1-800-829-3676. I find Publication 560 and the Internal Revenue Code invaluable sources to research questions and compliance issues regarding retirement plans.

In the back of this book you will find a glossary and an index. Hopefully, the glossary will provide a quick understanding of some of the terms used in this book. The index lists some of the most common topics and the pages on which they can be found (as indexes tend to do).

Finally, I would like to acknowledge the fact that this book would not be possible without the help of many authors and lecturers whose books and seminars I have studied. Over the course of many years, all of these have had a tremendous impact on my life and work. In particular, the discussions and ideas of Judy Tarpley and Susan Diehl of PenServ, Inc. were invaluable in developing the methodology used to create this book, and continue to be guiding forces in my field.

# Table of Contents

# CHAPTER I

*Introduction to Tax-Advantaged Plans*

# Chapter I

## *Introduction to Tax-Advantaged Plans*

For many years Congress has recognized that saving for retirement is a worthwhile social objective that should be encouraged by government. Retirement plans have actually been available for many years. Through the use of various tax incentives, the federal government has encouraged the growth of private pension and profit-sharing plans. Millions of companies have adopted them because they enable the company to save taxes and the employees to accumulate money for retirement. The widespread adoption of tax-advantaged retirement plans by both large and small businesses is its own testimonial to the attractiveness of such plans. However, the complexity of the tax laws governing these plans have often discouraged employers, especially the small business employer, from establishing these types of plans. The purpose of this book is to simplify these rules and regulations in order to help the business owner or manager understand the extraordinary benefits of these types of programs. After all, the most important aspect of any business is the *bottom line*. These types of plans can have a significant and positive impact on that bottom line. A tax-advantaged retirement plan is an invaluable tool in any business for enhancing revenue.

A retirement plan can be adopted by a business whether it operates as a corporation, a subchapter S corporation, a partnership, or a sole proprietorship. Once the objectives to be achieved have been determined, then a plan can be selected to help fulfill them. There are many types of tax-advantaged plans to choose from. For example:

## Defined Benefit Plans

A defined benefit plan is what most people think of as a "pension" plan. The benefit is defined in a formula, and contributions are made every year on a regular basis to accumulate a sum of money in order to be able to pay that benefit.

## Defined Contribution Plans

The trademark of a defined contribution plan is that the annual contribution is determined by a formula, and the ultimate benefit depends upon the investment returns of the plan:

### *Profit-Sharing Plans*

The most common defined contribution plan is the profit-sharing plan, such as a "Keogh" plan. Generally, contributions are the same percentage of each employee's compensation. These plans permit the company to make contributions as a defined percentage of profits and contributions can be skipped, reduced, or changed from year to year.

### *Money Purchase Pension Plans*

A companion plan to the profit-sharing plan is the money purchase pension plan. Contributions are determined by using a fixed formula based on a percentage of compensation, and the ultimate benefit depends strongly on the plan's earnings.

### *Target Benefit Plan*

The target benefit plan calculates a fixed annual contribution amount based on actuarial assumptions. A target benefit plan allocates contributions to separate participant accounts and the value at retirement is based on the investment growth in the account.

### 401(k) Plans

The *Cash or Deferred Arrangement (CODA)*, most commonly referred to as a 401(k) plan allows contributions to come from employees, rather than the company. Through salary reduction agreements, employees elect to reduce their salaries by a certain percentage and that amount is contributed to their accounts in the plan.

### Simplified Employee Pension (SEP) Plans

To establish a SEP, employees set up Individual Retirement Accounts (IRAs) into which the employer makes contributions. Once the contribution is placed in the employee's account, it belongs to the employee.

### Salary Reduction SEP (SAR-SEP) Plans

These plans enable an employer to establish a salary deferral plan [somewhat similar to a 401(k)], using the simplified adoption procedure of a SEP. This plan is limited to companies with 25 or fewer eligible employees and at least 50% of the eligible employees must elect to participate.

## Financial Security

Financial security is one reason many people become business owners. Of course, it is also the primary reason why most employees are even working. However, for many Americans in the workforce today, financial security is increasingly more difficult to obtain. Taxes reduce what an individual can save now, while inflation practically guarantees that even more money will be needed later.

What can a person do?  It is certainly not practical to try to change the tax laws and the hard realities of retirement will always exist.  But there are ways to reduce current taxes and help plan for a secure retirement.

## Three Ways to Take Money Out of a Business

If an owner of a business wants to take money out of the business, he* has three options:

♦   taking the money out as dividends from a corporation
♦   taking it as a salary
♦   taking the money and putting it into a qualified retirement plan

While the first two options may sound good, the tax consequences could change anyone's mind.  For example, assume that an individual wanted to take $25,000 from his business.  The table on the following page shows what would be netted under the three options.  Taxes dramatically reduce the share in all but the third option.  Why?

### Qualified Plans are Tax-Deferred

Money in a qualified retirement plan is not taxed until withdrawn.  This means that 100% of an individual's money is working for him, compounding free of taxes until withdrawn. Qualified plans are a great way to take money out of the business and allow both the owner and the employees to save for retirement.

---

* Throughout this book, I use the words "he, him, himself," etc. in their everyday androgynous sense of "he or she, him or her," etc... because the alternatives tend to produce tedious reading.

# Tax Facts of Taking Money out of a Business

|  | Corporate Dividend | Salary/ Income | Qualified Plan |
|---|---|---|---|
| **Profits** | $25,000 | $25,000 | $25,000 |
| **Corporate Tax** | $3,750 | $0 | $0 |
| **Personal Tax** | $9,000 | $9,000 | $0 |
| **Net After Tax** | $12,250 | $16,000 | $25,000 |

Assumptions: 15% corporate tax rate; 36% individual tax rate

It is no wonder that millions of employers have used the tax saving benefits available to them in retirement plans to build a strong foundation for the financial future of their employees *and themselves*.

Since all good things have limits and restrictions, the following chapters of this book will seek to explain, in a very simplified manner, the rules and regulations governing these types of tax-advantaged plans.

Whether an employer's objectives are to get the largest tax deduction on a contribution possible, to provide a program for employees' retirement, or to pass the costs of contributions on to employees through a salary deferral arrangement, there is a plan that is right for every business.

# CHAPTER II

*The Two Basic Categories of Employer Sponsored Plans*

# Chapter II

## *The Two Basic Categories of Employer Sponsored Plans*

### What is a Qualified Plan?

A Qualified Plan refers to a retirement plan which meets the formal requirements of Section 401(a) of the Internal Revenue Code. Therefore, a Qualified Plan is said to be "Qualified under Section 401(a)". Qualified Plans may be either profit-sharing, stock bonus, or pension plans. Since the enactment of the Employee Retirement Income Security Act of 1974 (ERISA), the terms "defined benefit plan" and "defined contribution plan" are also used to classify retirement plans. Following is a brief explanation of the major distinguishing features of each type of plan.

### Defined Benefit Plans

A defined benefit plan is a form of retirement plan in which the benefit is expressed as a certain amount which will be paid at the participant's retirement. The benefit to be received at retirement is specified by a definite formula and can therefore be determined at any point in time. For example, a plan that provides $1,000 per month to every retiring participant is a defined benefit plan, as is a plan which provides that each retiring employee will be paid an amount equal to four percent of his average annual compensation multiplied by his years of service with the company. The benefit formula usually bears some relationship to compensation and/or service with the employer. All defined benefit plans are thus pension plans which provide definitely determinable benefits.

Because a defined benefit plan promises a certain benefit to an employee at retirement, the employer is responsible for contributing to the plan the amount of funds necessary to pay benefits when they are due. An actuary must be retained to determine what dollar level of contribution is necessary. The actuary must make several assumptions, the most important of which is the rate of return on the investments made with the plan contributions and the rate of future salary increases of the participants. If the investments perform better than the actuary has assumed or if salaries do not increase as expected, the actual amount of contributions necessary from the employer is reduced. Conversely, if the investments do not perform as well as the actuary has assumed or if salaries increase faster than assumed, the employer must make up the difference through higher contributions.

**Defined Contribution Plans**

Defined contribution plans do not promise specific benefits. The plan benefit provided is instead based upon the amount that is contributed on behalf of each participant. Defined contribution plans are those in which funds contributed on behalf of each participant are accounted for separately and paid to him at retirement. For example, a profit-sharing plan is a defined contribution plan. So is a type of pension plan called a "money purchase" plan. A money purchase plan is one in which the employer promises to contribute a certain percentage of each participant's annual compensation to the plan each year. A money purchase plan is a pension plan with definitely determinable contributions. *(The money purchase plan acquires its name from the fact that at retirement, the **money*** *accumulated for each participant is often used to **purchase** an annuity contract for him).*

In a defined contribution plan, an account is established for each participant to record the accumulation of amounts contributed on his behalf and the account's share of earnings or losses made through the investment of the plan funds. The benefit that each employee ultimately receives is based upon his account balance. Individual account balances consist of contributions, investment gains or losses, and forfeitures, if any. This means that a participant's retirement value could vary from year to year depending on contributions and investment earnings gained over the life of the plan.

## Structural Classifications

While the two principal structural classifications of qualified plans are *Defined Benefit* and *Defined Contribution*, each particular classification has several characteristics peculiar to itself as well as several common characteristics. Below is a chart which outlines the structural classifications.

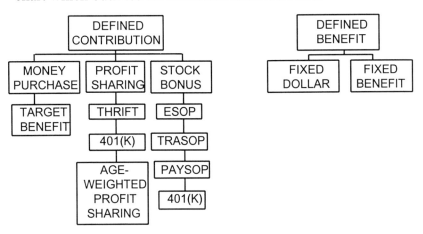

Because defined benefit plans often prove to be cost prohibitive to the small and medium sized business due to the actuarial requirements, this book will deal primarily with defined contribution plans. Therefore, in the chapters that follow, we will be taking a closer look at the similarities and differences between the different types of defined contribution plans. Those plans include the qualified plans shown on the left side of the preceding chart as well as Simplified Employee Pension (SEP) Plans, Salary Reduction SEP (SAR-SEP) Plans, and Savings Incentive Match Plans for Employees (SIMPLE Plans).

# CHAPTER III

*Simplified Employee*
*Pension Plans*
*(SEPs)*

# Chapter III

## *Simplified Employee Pension Plans (SEPs)*

T he Simplified Employee Pension Plan, or SEP (most commonly pronounced as a word, "Sep"), is an easy and economical plan to establish and administer. A SEP is simply another method of funding an IRA. Under this plan, an employer makes contributions directly to IRAs set up by eligible employees. A SEP can be used by any business, whether a corporation, partnership, or sole proprietorship. The sole owner of a business can also establish a SEP for himself. The owner of the business is also considered an employee who is eligible to receive a SEP contribution. Up to the lesser of 15% of compensation or $30,000 can be deposited annually to a SEP for an eligible employee. However, only up to $150,000 of compensation (as indexed for inflation; for 1997 that number changes to $160,000) can be considered in calculating the contribution.

An employee who receives a SEP contribution can also make a regular IRA contribution of up to the lesser of 100% of compensation or $2,000. However, participation in a SEP constitutes "active participation in an employer sponsored plan." Therefore, a regular IRA contribution may or may not be tax deductible (see Chapter XII for IRA deductibility rules).

Unlike regular IRAs where the plan must be established and funded by April 15 of the following year, an employer has until the due date of the federal income tax return of the business, *including extensions*, to establish and make SEP contributions.

In order to establish a SEP, an employer must adopt a plan by signing a written agreement. This instrument must include the name of the employer, the requirements for participation, and a definite formula for allocation of contributions. The amounts which will be contributed to the SEP may be determined annually by the employer and are not required to be made each year.

Another requirement for SEP establishment is 100% participation by all eligible employees. That is, all eligible employees must establish IRAs. An eligible employee may not waive out of receiving an employer contribution. The employer is also required to provide each employee with information about the SEP plan. Generally, if the IRS Form 5305-SEP or a prototype is used, this means providing employee with an executed copy of the agreement. The employees should also receive a SEP disclosure explanation which details the general SEP rules and provisions of the plan.

An employer may set certain eligibility requirements when adopting a SEP. However, there are rules that have been set limiting the restrictiveness of those requirements. For example, part-time employees may not be excluded. If an employee earns at least $400 (1997 figure, indexed) in a year, he must be included if the other eligibility requirements are met.

Employees under the age of 21 may be excluded. An employer may also require that an employee work for the business for up to 3 of the last 5 years (an employee receives credit for one year if he works only one day during such year). An employer is not required to cover an employee who is a non-resident alien.

The SEP can be an attractive retirement planning option, especially to the small business owner, where a profit-sharing or 401(k) plan may be too costly or difficult to administer.

## Contribution Rules

Once the plan has been established, it is the employer who is responsible for determining whether an employee has met the eligibility requirements and is eligible to receive a contribution. The contributions must be uniform: Employer contributions under a SEP plan must bear a uniform relationship to the compensation of each employee covered under the SEP plan. In other words, if the business owner contributes 15% of his compensation, each eligible employee must also receive a contribution of 15% of their compensation from the employer. As previously mentioned, the maximum contribution to a SEP is limited to the lesser of 15% of compensation or $30,000 per tax year *(Although, under the new rules for calculating the contribution beginning 1/1/94, mathematically only up to $22,500 can be contributed, not the statutory limit of $30,000. This is due to a compensation cap, for calculation purposes, of $150,000 indexed for inflation in $10,000 increments created by the Omnibus Budget Reconciliation Act of 1993; See Appendix).*

**If an employer contributes too much:** Any employer contribution which exceeds the allocation formula for the year is treated as a regular IRA contribution made by the employee. **In no event** may an employer who over-contributes to an employee's IRA under a SEP plan get the money back from the employee's IRA. This excess amount is considered to be additional compensation paid to the employee by the employer for W-2 purposes.

Once again, this additional amount is treated as a regular IRA contribution made by the employee. Where this amount, when added to the individual's other regular IRA contributions for the year, exceeds the $2,000 regular IRA contribution limit, an IRA excess is created. The individual would be subject to a 6% excess contribution penalty if the person does not withdraw the excess plus the earnings attributable no later than his tax filing deadline for the year, including extensions.

**Total Flexibility:** An employer has total flexibility from year to year in determining the percentage of compensation to be contributed into each employee's IRA. It can range anywhere from 0% to 15% and vary each year. The only requirement placed upon the employer is that the employer must determine in writing each year his "allocation formula." This information is required to be communicated to each employee.

An employer's **deduction** for contributions to a SEP is limited to 15% of each eligible employee's compensation and is taken on the business income tax return. However, for a non-incorporated business, the business owner's own SEP contribution is deducted on his own Form 1040, not on the business return.

Keep in mind that a SEP is simply another method of funding an IRA. Therefore, most of the rules governing SEPs are IRA rules. Because of this, a SEP plan is an extremely simple retirement plan to get started. SEPs are becoming more and more attractive, especially to the small to medium-sized companies. SEPs are being called "The Small Business Retirement Plan of the 90's."

# CHAPTER IV

*Salary Reduction*
*Simplified Employee*
*Pension Plans (SAR-SEPs)*

# Chapter IV

## *Salary Reduction Simplified Employee Pension Plans (SAR-SEPs)*

The Tax Reform Act of 1986 added a new feature to the SEP which provided employers an option to allow their employees to contribute to their own SEP accounts through a salary reduction program. Thus, a SEP can become even more flexible and offer features similar to a 401(k) plan. Through a salary reduction program, an employee can instruct his employer to withhold a portion of his compensation up to the lesser of 15% of compensation or $7,000 and deposit it directly to his SEP account (The $7,000 limitation on elective deferrals is indexed annually based on cost of living adjustments as required by the Internal Revenue Code §402(g)(5); the actual figure for 1997 is $9,500). The amount of the contribution reduces the employee's taxable compensation.

For example, if an employee earns $30,000 a year and elects to defer 5% ($1,500) to the SAR-SEP, the taxable income for the employee would be reduced to $28,500. The employee's deferral can be coordinated with the employer's SEP contribution provided that the sum of the two does not exceed the lesser of 15% of compensation or $30,000.

A business is not required to have a profit in order for elective deferrals to be made to the SEP.

## _Eligibility_

The business must have had 25 or fewer employees eligible to participate, including the employer, at all times during the prior year. New employers who had no employees during the prior year will meet this requirement if they have 25 or fewer employees eligible to participate throughout the first 30 days that the employer's business is in existence.

At least 50% of the total number of employees eligible to participate must elect to have amounts contributed to the SAR-SEP.

The average amount of salary reduction contributions made on behalf of highly compensated employees eligible to participate in the SAR-SEP cannot exceed 1.25 times the average amount of salary reduction contributions made on behalf of all eligible employees other than those who are highly compensated.

> Prior to 1997, the definition of a _highly compensated employee_ for retirement plans was very complex with different rules applying to the current year and the "look back" years. The new definitions beginning January 1, 1997 for the highly compensated employee will include the following:
>
> 1. A person who owns more than 5% of the business at any time during the year; or
>
> 2. Anyone who, during the preceding year, had compensation in excess of $80,000 (subject to cost of living adjustments) and was in the top-paid group for the year. The top-paid group will include the top 20% of the employees ranked in order of compensation.

This repeals the rule that the highest paid officers are automatically deemed to be highly compensated employees.

Additional information regarding changes to retirement plans beginning in 1997 can be found in the appendix to this book under the heading, "Small Business Job Protection Act of 1996. This Act created the SIMPLE plan, discussed later.

Although salary deferral SEPs are very similar to 401(k)s, they are different in a very important way. While §401(k) plans allow an employer to make a matching contribution for the benefit of employees making salary deferrals, matching contributions are not permitted in a SAR-SEP.

Employees who defer part of their salary under a SAR-SEP reduce their gross income by the amount of the deferral. Therefore, elective deferrals are not taxable to the employee. Furthermore, elective deferrals are *tax deductible* to the employer. Note, however, the elective deferrals are subject to FICA taxes.

The SAR-SEP is a simple way to provide a retirement plan for employees. SEPs are relatively easy to administer compared to qualified plans because the current reporting requirements for qualified plans do not apply to SEPs. The SAR-SEP is less expensive than a qualified plan and generally less complicated to establish because most of the SEP rules are IRA rules. *However, the SAR-SEP is somewhat more complicated than a regular SEP because it deals with elective deferrals and must meet certain non-discrimination tests.*

SAR-SEPs may be especially attractive to employers who want to offer a retirement plan as an incentive for employees but who want to avoid the expense of establishing and administering a qualified plan.

**Important Note:** As a result of the Small Business Job Protection Act of 1996, the provisions in the tax code for the establishment of new SAR-SEPs are being repealed. Beginning January 1, 1997, SAR-SEPs will no longer be available except for those employers who had a SAR-SEP in place prior to 1997. This Act created a new type of retirement plan known as a "SIMPLE" plan. SIMPLE is an acronym for **S**avings **I**ncentive **M**atch **PL**an for **E**mployees and is discussed in detail in another chapter of this book.

# CHAPTER V

*"Keogh" Plans*

# Chapter V

## *"Keogh" Plans*

Named after Eugene Keogh, the U.S. Congressman from New York who introduced the legislation that created them, the *Keogh* was originally a special program of tax incentives for retirement planning by the self-employed (Judy Tarpley, Vice President and co-founder of PenServ, Inc. a national pension design and consulting firm, jokingly refers to "KEOGH" as an acronym for *Keep Earnings Out of Government Hands!*). After the enactment of the Self-Employed Individuals Retirement Act of 1962, the program went into effect in 1963. The law permits self-employed individuals to establish, or participate in, qualified pension and profit sharing plans similar to those of large corporations.

The Tax Equity and Fiscal Responsibility Act of 1982 (TEFRA) substantially changed the structure of Keogh plans. TEFRA generally eliminated the distinction in the tax law between qualified plans of corporations and those of self-employed individuals. In general, TEFRA repealed many of the special rules for self-employed plans (including the special limits on contributions and deductions), extended some of the rules to all qualified plans, and applied some of the repealed rules, with modifications, to plans of corporate and non-corporate employers which primarily benefit key employees which are referred to as "top-heavy" plans.

We now use the term "Keogh" generically to describe a qualified plan established by an unincorporated business. If an individual works for himself, or owns a business or part of a business, a Keogh Plan merits consideration. However, the individual must actually perform personal services for the business. Mere passive investments are not enough to constitute self-employment.

By establishing a Keogh plan, a business owner can reduce his taxable income each year by as much as $30,000! In addition, the contribution to the plan, plus the earnings on those contributions continue to grow in the account tax-deferred until withdrawn.

Under a Keogh plan, each year a contribution and deduction may be made of up to 25% of an individual's annual *earned income* up to $30,000, completely tax-deferred.

Generally, *earned income* is not the same as "Net Profit" from your trade or business. Beginning January 1, 1994, only the first $150,000 (to be indexed for inflation) of an individual's earned income may be used in calculating the contribution. The actual amount that may be deducted for contributions to a Keogh Plan depends on the type of Keogh Plan adopted.

## Types of Keogh Plans

### Profit Sharing

A Profit Sharing Keogh allows the business owner to select each year the percent of his earned income to be contributed to the plan. There is no obligation to contribute the same percentage each year. However, the maximum annual deduction is 15% of earned income or $30,000, whichever is the lesser amount.

## *Money Purchase Pension*

A Money Purchase Pension Keogh allows the business owner to select a fixed percentage of his earned income to be contributed every year. The maximum annual contribution and deduction is limited to the lesser of 25% of earned income or $30,000.

## *Combination Plans*

To get the maximum flexibility and annual deduction, an individual can combine a Profit Sharing and a Money Purchase Pension Plan. For example, by adopting a combination of these plans, an individual might elect to contribute 10% each year of his earned income to a Money Purchase Plan and have the option to contribute up to 15% of his earned income to the Profit Sharing Plan. However, the total amount contributed to both plans cannot exceed the lesser of 25% of earned income or $30,000 each year.

A taxpayer must establish a Keogh plan no later than his tax year-end (December 31st for calendar year businesses) for which the initial contribution and deduction will be made. However, the individual will have until his tax filing deadline (usually April 15th of the following year) plus any extensions to make the contribution to the plan and still be able to deduct the contribution on the tax return.

Since the distinctions in the tax law for incorporated and unincorporated businesses have been eliminated, as previously mentioned, the following chapters on Profit Sharing and Money Purchase Pension Plans will go into greater detail on these plans and may be applied to the "Keogh" as well.

# CHAPTER VI

*Profit-Sharing*
*Plans*

# Chapter VI

## *Profit-Sharing Plans*

A *Profit-Sharing Plan* is a "discretionary contribution" plan established by an employer to provide for the participation in the employer's profits by the employees. The plan document must provide for a definite predetermined formula for allocating the contributions made to the plan. The amount of the contribution may be determined each year by the employer and is limited to 15% of total compensation each year. It is not necessary any longer to base contributions on the existence of current or accumulated profits.

Profit-sharing plans allow for contribution flexibility. The amount of the contribution can vary from year to year depending on the financial condition of the company. If a company experiences a year with little or no profits, no contributions are required. Profit-sharing plans may also stimulate employees to be more productive, thus resulting in greater profits for both the company and for themselves.

### Tax Advantages

Profit-sharing plans have tax advantages similar to those available to qualified pension plans under the federal Internal Revenue Code. Within certain limits, the employer may deduct for federal income tax purposes the contributions that he makes to the profit-sharing fund. The employees' respective shares of these contributions are not taxable to the employees at the time they are made by the employer, but are taxable to the employees at the time they receive them as distributions from the plan.

## Advantages Under ERISA

In addition to tax advantages, a profit-sharing plan has the advantage of being relieved from compliance with some of the most stringent demands of the Employee Retirement Income Security Act of 1974. Profit-sharing plans are not subject to the funding standards of ERISA and are not required to comply with the termination insurance requirements of that law. However, profit-sharing plans are subject to the participation and vesting standards of ERISA and must adhere to the exacting fiduciary, reporting, and disclosure requirements of that law.

## Account Balances

When a profit-sharing plan is adopted, an account is established for each participant to record the amounts held in the plan for his benefit. The total balance of all participants' accounts equals the total amount in the plan. The actual funds may be pooled together and invested by the trustees or the participants may be given the right to direct the investments in their own accounts. Each participant's benefit is based upon all or a portion of his account balance. A popular type of profit-sharing plan, which has special additional rules, is the Cash or Deferred Arrangement (CODA), discussed in Chapter VIII.

## Allocation of Contributions

The employer contribution, once determined, is allocated among the participant's accounts. It is usually allocated based upon the relative compensation of the participants for the year. In other words, the amount allocated to a participant whose compensation is $20,000 will equal half of the amount allocated to a participant whose compensation is $40,000. Virtually any allocation method which does not discriminate in favor of the highly compensated employees, however, is permitted (The regulations provide general testing methods to prove non-discrimination).

## Maximum Allocations

For a defined contribution plan, such as a profit-sharing plan, to be qualified, the "annual additions" allocated to any one participant's account cannot exceed the lesser of 25 percent of his compensation or $30,000 [The $30,000 limit will not be increased annually for cost-of-living adjustments due to a recent amendment to the Internal Revenue Code. However, many profit-sharing plans limit the employer's annual contribution limit on behalf of any participant to the lesser of *15% of compensation or $30,000*, which corresponds to the employer's deductible limit under the profit-sharing rules.

*Note: As explained in Appendix A at the end of this book, the Omnibus Budget Reconciliation Act of 1993 reduced the maximum amount of compensation to be used in the calculation to $150,000 beginning in 1994. As a result, in some cases, the $30,000 overall limit will not be reached by a participant.*

"Annual additions" include the employer's contributions, forfeitures, and the employee's contributions, if any. These rules must be followed in order for the profit-sharing plan to be considered a "qualified plan" and thus receive the special tax advantages.

## Benefits

A participant's benefit under a profit-sharing plan is derived from his account balance for the employer's contributions plus forfeitures and his account balance for his own contributions, if any. The earnings and losses of the trust are also allocated to his account at least annually as adjustments to the account balance. Upon becoming eligible for a benefit under the plan, the participant will receive his *vested* portion of the amount in his account (vesting rules are discussed in Chapter XXII).

## Distributions

The distribution of account balances in a profit-sharing plan is generally made by payment in a lump sum, installments, or the purchase of an annuity contract for the benefit of the participants.

The time at which the distribution of the account balance is actually made to a participant depends upon the terms of the plan. The Code sets forth rules regarding the latest time benefits must commence. In general, the plan must provide that a participant's benefit will be paid to him, unless he "elects otherwise," no later than sixty days after the end of the plan year in which the *latest* of the following events occurs:

- The date on which he attains the age of 65 (or the plan's normal retirement age, if earlier);

- The tenth anniversary of the year in which he commenced participation in the plan; or

- The date on which he terminates service with the employer.

Most profit-sharing plans, however, permit the distribution of benefits within a short time after an employee has terminated employment, becomes disabled, or dies. In cases in which the account balance is not immediately distributed, it must be credited with the trust's investment earnings or losses until it is actually paid.

Even though qualified profit-sharing plans are a form of retirement plan since they defer the payment of amounts contributed on behalf of participants to a later date, a profit-sharing plan may distribute amounts contributed as long as such amounts have been in the plan for two years. The two year period begins when the contribution is actually made to the plan's trust. A profit-sharing plan may also allow employees with five years of participation to withdraw all employer contributions. Most large plans permit withdrawals only for specified reasons (such as the need for funds to purchase a primary residence, pay for a child's college expenses, or to defray large catastrophic medical expenses). However, a participant must often pay a penalty tax to the IRS on any taxable distribution of funds if the distribution is made prior to the participant attaining the age of 59½.

# CHAPTER VII

*Money Purchase*
*Pension Plans*

# Chapter VII

## *Money Purchase Pension Plans*

A money purchase plan is often a great companion plan to the profit sharing plan. Contributions are determined by using a fixed formula based on a percentage of compensation, and the ultimate benefit depends strongly on the plan's earnings.

In a money purchase pension plan, the employer selects a specified percentage of current compensation which it will contribute. Unlike a profit sharing plan, the amount must be contributed each year, regardless of company profits; there is really no contribution flexibility unless the plan is amended.

Money purchase plans also bear a resemblance to profit sharing plans. Like a profit sharing plan, an account is established for each participant to record the contributions made for him.

**Tax Advantages**

Within certain limits, the employer may deduct for federal income tax purposes the contributions that he makes to the money purchase pension plan. The employees' respective shares of these contributions are not taxable to the employees at the time they are made by the employer, but are taxable to the employees at the time they receive them as distributions from the plan.

## Account Balances

When a Money purchase pension plan is adopted, an account is established for each participant to record the amounts held in the plan for his benefit. The total balance of all participants' accounts equals the total amount in the plan. The actual funds may be pooled together and invested by the trustees or the participants may be given the right to direct the investments in their own accounts. Each participant's benefit is based upon all or a portion of his account balance.

## Allocation of Contributions

The employer contribution, once determined, is allocated among the participant's accounts. It is usually allocated based upon the relative compensation of the participants for the year. In other words, the amount allocated to a participant whose compensation is $25,000 will equal half of the amount allocated to a participant whose compensation is $50,000. Virtually any allocation method which does not discriminate in favor of the highly compensated employees, however, is permitted (The regulations provide general testing methods to prove non-discrimination).

A money purchase plan is a pension plan and therefore contributions do not necessarily come from profits of the company, but rather represent a fixed commitment to be met, regardless of whether or not the company is profitable. It acquires its name from the fact that at retirement, the *money* accumulated for each participant is often used to *purchase* an annuity contract for him. The plan states the employer's contribution, usually expressed as a percentage of each participant's compensation, but may be a fixed dollar amount (not to exceed 25% of compensation for any employee). For example, a plan may provide that each year the employer will contribute to the plan an amount equal to ten percent of each participant's compensation. Although any amount the employer fixes as a contribution rate must be contributed and is 100% deductible by the company, the percentage the employer chooses to contribute cannot be more than 25 percent. In other words, whatever fixed contribution formula (percentage of compensation or dollar amount) is selected by the employer on the adoption agreement not only becomes the employer's required contribution for the year, but it also becomes the employer's deduction limit.

## Maximum Allocations

For a defined contribution plan, such as a Money Purchase Pension Plan, to be qualified, the "annual additions" allocated to any one participant's account cannot exceed the lesser of 25 percent of his compensation or $30,000.

"Annual additions" include the employer's contributions, forfeitures, and the employee's contributions, if any. These rules must be followed in order for the money purchase pension plan to be considered a "qualified plan" and thus receive the special tax advantages.

## Benefits

Like a profit sharing plan, a participant's benefit under a money purchase pension plan is derived from his account balance for the employer's contributions plus forfeitures and his account balance for his own contributions, if any. The earnings and losses of the trust are also allocated to his account at least annually as adjustments to the account balance. Upon becoming eligible for a benefit under the plan, the participant will receive his *vested* portion of the amount in his account (vesting rules are discussed in Chapter XXII).

## Distributions

Unlike the case with a profit sharing plan, because a money purchase plan is a pension plan, distributions prior to the participant's termination of employment are not permitted. Keep in mind the purpose Congress intended when it created the pension plan: to provide livelihood at retirement. Therefore, a participant may not withdraw any portion of his account balance while the employee is still working for the company. Furthermore, employees terminating participation in a money purchase pension plan are often (but not always) not given distributions of their account balances until they reach the plan's normal retirement age. However, like a profit sharing plan, a money purchase pension plan provides for 100 percent vesting and immediate distribution if a participant becomes disabled or dies while employed.

# CHAPTER VIII

*401(k) Plans-
Cash or Deferred
Arrangements
(CODAs)*

# Chapter VIII

## *401(k) Plans- Cash or Deferred Arrangements (CODAs)*

The term "40l(k) plan" refers to a specific section of the Internal Revenue Code which authorizes a unique type of employee benefit plan. These plans are commonly referred to as "cash or deferred arrangements" or CODAs, and allow participants to voluntarily reduce their current income before taxation and have their employer contribute the amount reduced to the plan.

The unique feature of a 401(k) plan is that it permits an employee to elect between (1) having his employer contribute a portion of his salary to a 401(k) plan on his behalf, and (2) having the employer pay the amount directly to him. The important advantage of the plan is that if the money is contributed to the plan, the employee is not currently taxed on it for federal income tax purposes.

In order to qualify under Section 401(k), the plan must first qualify as a profit-sharing or stock bonus plan under Section 401(a) of the Code. Qualification is also subject to passage of strict non-discrimination tests to insure that the plan does not discriminate in favor of the highly compensated employees. Further, restrictions on withdrawals must limit access by a participant to his account to the attainment of age 59½, death, disability, termination of employment, or financial hardship.

All contributions are considered to be employer contributions since they are handled as payroll reductions rather than direct payments from the participant. Contributions are also subject to the overall maximum contribution allowable under a qualified retirement plan.

## Legislative Background

In 1978, Section 401(k) was added to the Internal Revenue Code allowing qualified status to certain "cash or deferred arrangements" under employee plans. Specifically, it allowed employees either to take company profit sharing allocations, bonuses, or salaries in cash immediately, or to defer receipt until a later date.

Previously, plans which offered the option of taking the cash immediately or deferring it were subject to taxation whether or not the actual receipt of the cash was immediate or deferred. Under Section 401(k) and the subsequent proposed regulations, the amount taken in cash is immediately taxable, but the amount deferred is not. This represents a dramatic change in the understanding of constructive receipt in these arrangements, which has created the unique status of a 401(k) plan.

The requirements of Section 401(k) have been further modified by the Tax Reform Act of 1986 and subsequent regulations issued in August, 1988. These modifications are reflected in the description of the plan options provided below.

## Types of 401(k) Arrangements

In most situations, 401(k) arrangements are offered as an option under an existing profit-sharing or stock bonus plan, although they may be offered on a stand-alone basis.

There are three basic types of plans available under Section 401(k):

*Cash Option Plans* - These plans allow employees the option of taking employer profit-sharing allocations and/or bonuses either in cash or as tax deferred contributions to the plan.

*Salary Reduction Plans* - In this type of plan, employees are allowed to voluntarily reduce their salary and to have their employer contribute the amount of the reduction to the plan as an employer contribution.

*Salary Reduction/Matching Plan* - Similar to Salary Reduction Plans, these plans provide the employee an additional incentive to participate by providing employer matching contributions equal to all or part of the amount contributed by the employee.

All of the above plans have similar advantages, restrictions and problems.

**Advantages of 401(k)**

Interest in 401(k) programs is widespread. Many employers have, are, or will be, considering establishing a 401(k) program in the near future. Employee pressure, competition, and the desire to improve employee benefits at a reasonable cost are all important reasons for the high level of interest. Other advantages of the program include:

> *Participant Tax Savings* - Not only are federal income taxes deferred until the contributions and any earnings are actually distributed, but there may be further savings through favorable tax averaging treatment at time of distribution.

*IRA Replacement* - the Tax Reform Act of 1986 placed restrictions on those employees who are eligible to make deductible IRA contributions. If an employee or his spouse is covered by a qualified retirement plan, he will not be permitted to make deductible IRA contributions if their income exceeds a certain threshold. The 401(k) plan can be used to provide the employee a means of replacing the before-tax contributions which have previously been made to an IRA.

*Employee Recruitment* - A 401(k) plan is widely recognized as a beneficial program and thus gives the employer an additional tool for recruiting and retaining key employees.

*Employer Contributions* - Contributions made by the Employer up to the maximum amount specified in the Internal Revenue Code are 100% deductible as an ordinary and necessary business expense.

## Eligibility and Participation Requirements

*Age and Service Requirements* - Any Employee who has completed at least one year of service and attained age 21 must be eligible to participate in the plan. A *year of service* is defined as a 12 month period of employment during which the employee works 1,000 hours or more. Consequently, the Plan can establish a minimum age and /or service requirement to be completed by an employee before he is permitted to join the Plan, but the age requirement cannot exceed age 21 and the service requirement cannot exceed one year of service.

*Coverage Requirements* - The Internal Revenue Code provides that a 401(k) Plan cannot discriminate in favor of "Highly Compensated Employees" (see definition below). In order to

72

meet this standard with regard to plan coverage, the plan must satisfy one of the following tests:

(1) **_70% Test:_** The ratio of non-highly compensated employees eligible to participate to the highly compensated employees eligible to participate must be at least 70%, **or**

(2) **_Average Benefits Test:_** The employees eligible to participate in the plan must represent a "fair cross-section" of all employees and the average benefit available to non-highly compensated employees must be at least 70% of the average benefit available to highly compensated employees.

In determining those employees who are eligible to participate for purposes of these tests, those employees who have not satisfied the age and service requirement may be disregarded.

**Contribution Requirements**

*Employee Elective Contributions* - Each participating employee may elect to reduce his compensation and have such amount contributed to the Plan. The Plan can provide for a minimum level, a maximum level, and a stated increment such as "from 2% to 10% of compensation in multiples of 1%". Each Employee is limited to a maximum Elective Contribution of the lesser of 25% of compensation or $7,000 per year (indexed for inflation; the 1997 figure is actually $9,500).

*Employer Matching Contribution* - The employer may elect to match a portion or all of the Employee Elective Contributions. The employer may establish the rate of the matching contribution and the maximum amount to be matched on an annual basis. For example, the employer might provide a contribution of $.50 for each $1 of

Employee Elective Contributions to a maximum Employee Elective Contribution of 5% of compensation.

*Employer Discretionary Contribution* - In addition to the Matching Contribution, the Employer may elect to contribute an additional discretionary amount to be allocated among all employees who have satisfied the age and service requirements for the plan.

*Maximum Contribution* - The combined total of the Employee and Employer Contributions for all plan participants is subject to a maximum equal to 15 percent of the total compensation for all eligible plan participants. The maximum combined employee and employer contributions which can be made on behalf of any participant for a given year is the lesser of 25 percent of the participant's compensation or $30,000.

*Employee Contribution Nondiscrimination Test* - In order to be considered nondiscriminatory, the employee elective contributions must meet one of the Actual Deferral Percentage Tests described below.

(1) ***Actual Deferral Percentage Test 1*** - The average percentage of compensation deferred by the "highly compensated" employees cannot exceed 1.25 times the average percentage of compensation deferred by the "non-highly compensated" employees, *or*

(2) ***Actual Deferral Percentage Test 2*** - the average percentage of compensation deferred by the "highly compensated" employees cannot exceed by more than 2% the percentage of salary deferred by the "non-highly compensated" and the average percentage deferred by the "highly compensated" cannot exceed 2 times the average percentage deferred by the "non-highly compensated".

For purposes of Section 401(k), a "highly compensated" employee is an employee who in the current or prior year,

1.      Owns more than 5% of the business at any time during the year; or

2.      Anyone who, during the preceding year, had compensation in excess of $80,000 (subject to cost of living adjustments) and was in the top-paid group for the year. The top-paid group will include the top 20% of the employees ranked in order of compensation.

The 1996 Small Business Act repealed the rule that the highest paid officers are automatically deemed to be highly compensated employees.

*Top-Heavy* - A 401(k) plan is top-heavy if, as of the "determination date", the total of the accounts of all "key" employees exceeds 60% of the total of the accounts of all employees. The determination date for a new plan is the last day of the first plan year; for an existing plan, it is the last day of the preceding plan year. For purposes of Section 401(k), a "key" employee is an employee who, at any time during the plan year or any of the four preceding plan years, is (or was):

a. a 5% owner; or

b. a 1% owner whose annual compensation exceeds $150,000; or

c. an officer having annual compensation in excess of $45,000 (indexed for inflation, this is $60,000 in 1996).

If a plan is determined to be top-heavy, the employer's contribution for each non-key employee must not be less than the lesser of:

a. 3 percent of compensation; or

b. the highest contribution percentage rate for a key employee

## Normal Retirement

*Normal Retirement Age* - The Normal Retirement Age is the age at which a participant becomes eligible to retire and receive benefits from the Plan. This age is selected by the Employer, but cannot exceed age 65.

*Retirement Benefits* - At retirement, a Participant is entitled to receive the entire sum in his account applied under any of the following options:

a. A single sum payment.

b. Substantially equal periodic installments over a period not to exceed the life expectancy of the Participant.

c. A life annuity.

d. A joint and last survivor annuity.

## Limitation on Withdrawals and Distributions

A 401(k) plan must impose strict limitations upon the employee's right to withdraw amounts that were contributed to the plan on his behalf. The contributions and earnings thereon must not be distributable earlier than the occurrence of one of the following events:

1. Normal retirement
2. Death
3. Disability
4. Separation from service
5. Attainment of age 59 1/2, or
6. Financial hardship (only cumulative Employee Elective Contributions can be withdrawn).

## Benefits Upon Termination of Employment

Upon termination of employment prior to normal retirement age, the participant will always be 100% vested in his employee elective contributions and the earnings thereon. In addition, the participant may be entitled to some portion of the value of his employer contribution account, depending on the vesting schedule selected for the Plan. The employer is free to select a schedule from among several which meet IRS requirements. Some sample schedules have been listed below:

1. *Five Year Cliff Vesting*

| Years of Service | Vested Rate |
|---|---|
| Less than 5 | 0% |
| 5 or more | 100% |

2. *Seven Year Graded Vesting*

| Years of Service | Vested Rate |
|---|---|
| Less than 3 | 0% |
| 3 but less than 4 | 20% |
| 4 but less than 5 | 40% |
| 5 but less than 6 | 60% |
| 6 but less than 7 | 80% |
| 7 or more | 100% |

3. *Three Year Cliff Vesting*

| Years of Service | Vested Rate |
|---|---|
| Less than 3 | 0% |
| 3 or more | 100% |

4. *Six Year Graded Vesting*

| Years of Service | Vested Rate |
|---|---|
| Less than 2 | 0% |
| 2 but less than 3 | 20% |
| 3 but less than 4 | 40% |
| 4 but less than 5 | 60% |
| 5 but less than 6 | 80% |
| 6 or more | 100% |

If the plan is determined to be top-heavy, then vesting schedules 1 and 2 cannot be utilized.

**Tax Implication of Benefit Distribution**

*Federal Income Tax* - The general rule is that distributions attributable to Employer contributions and Employee Elective contributions will be taxed at ordinary income tax rates when received. However, there are several circumstances under which the participant may receive more favorable treatment.

*Five Year Averaging* - A lump sum distribution may qualify for special 5 year forward averaging treatment if the distribution is made because of death, disability, or following the attainment of age 59½.

*Direct Transfer or Rollover* - all or part of a lump sum distribution can be rolled directly into an Individual Retirement Account or another qualified retirement plan, and taxation is deferred until payments are made from the IRA or qualified plan. As of January 1, 1993, if the distribution is not rolled directly to an IRA or another qualified plan, then 20% of the distribution must be withheld for federal income tax.

## Trust Requirements and Trustee Obligations

*Selection of Trustee* - The Employer must select a trustee to manage and invest the plan assets. The trustee has the fiduciary obligation to operate the trust for the exclusive benefit of the plan Participants.

*Fiduciary Obligation* - Both the Internal Revenue Code and ERISA require that the trustee, as a plan fiduciary, discharge his duties solely in the interests of the participants and their beneficiaries. Some of the specific requirements are as follows:

- The fiduciary must act as would a "prudent man" in similar circumstances;
- The plan assets must be sufficiently diversified so as to minimize the risk of large losses;
- The plan must have sufficient liquidity; and
- The plan must yield a fair return commensurate with the prevailing rate.

## Investment Selection

Subject to the limitations discussed above, the trustees are charged with investing the plan assets. The trustees may permit the individual participants to direct the investment of their own plan account. The following are among the more common investment selections for plan assets:

- Selected portfolio of stocks, bonds and cash investments accounts;
- Mutual Funds;
- Private investments; and
- Certificates of Deposit and similar instruments.

## Loans to Participants

Since The Tax Reform Act of 1986 (TRA '86) imposed a 10% excise tax on early withdrawals (before age 59½), 401(k) plans have increasingly incorporated loan provisions. Such provisions allow participants to have access to their money, and thereby increase participation, particularly among young, lower-paid employees. If the employer so elects, loans can be made available to plan participants subject to the following restrictions:

1. The amount of the loan cannot exceed the lesser of:

   a. $50,000 or
   b. one-half (½) the present value of the Employee's non-forfeitable accrued benefit.

2. The loan must bear a reasonable rate of interest.

3. The loan must be adequately secured.

4. Loans must be made available on a non-discriminatory basis.

5. The loan must be repaid within 5 years with at least quarterly payments of principal and interest. However, the 5 year requirement is waived if the loan is used to acquire a dwelling which is to be the principal residence of the participant.

6. Loans must be repaid through payroll deduction.

401(k) plans are cost-effective for employers since the amount they must contribute is reduced by the contributions of participants. However, these plans are more difficult to administer than other types of defined contribution plans due to the special non-discrimination requirements and different funding limitations.

# CHAPTER IX

*Age-Weighted
Profit Sharing Plans*

# Chapter IX

## *Age-Weighted Profit Sharing Plans*

A ge-weighted profit-sharing plans erupted onto the scene in 1990 as a by-product of the proposed Internal Revenue Code Section 401(a)(4) regulations. At first, there was concern that this new plan design was not intended by the "cross-testing" provisions of the regulations. However, public pronouncements by various Internal Revenue Service officials stated that age-weighted profit sharing plans were permissible, and "had always been possible." The cross-testing provisions have remained in every version of the final regulations. However, there is still doubt among many that its permissibility will continue.

The age-weighted feature of the plan is closely akin to target benefit plans (to be discussed further in Chapter XI), with the added flexibility of discretionary profit sharing contributions. Similar to a defined benefit plan, the age-weighting provides for larger contributions for older employees because of the short accumulation period they have between the contribution age and the intended retirement age.

Up until a few years ago, the defined benefit plan was considered an excellent vehicle for the older principals of a firm because the benefit (i.e., contribution) was generally based on the age, service, and compensation of the individual.

Certain objections have recently scared employers away from defined benefit plans: full funding limits, fixed commitment, administrative fees, Pension Benefit Guaranty Corporation (PBGC) premiums, government intervention, reversion taxes, excise taxes, etc. While the defined benefit plan is certainly not dead, it is not always a popular plan because of the excessive regulatory climate that surrounds it.

This creates a problem: how to continue to meet the needs of the older, highly compensated principals without "overcompensating" the nonhighly compensated. The IRC Sec. 401(a)(4) regulations have provided the solution: the Age-Weighted Profit-Sharing Plan.

**Simple Explanation**

In simplest terms, an age-weighted profit-sharing plan is a target benefit plan (discussed in detail in Chapter XI) that is wrapped around a profit-sharing plan instead of a money purchase pension plan. The "fixed commitment" aspect of the money purchase plan has been removed, while preserving the age-weighting factor and the less onerous regulatory aspects of the defined contribution plan.

Allocations in a simple profit-sharing plan are based on the compensation of the individual participants. In an age-weighted profit-sharing plan, allocations are based on both individual compensation and the age of each participant. Age is one of the critical components for this type of plan to work properly.

If the final benefit accumulation is important to the client, it may be better to consider a defined benefit plan. When comparing a defined benefit plan to an age-weighted profit-sharing plan, three critical differences should be recognized:

(1) A profit-sharing plan cannot take into account past service, while a defined benefit plan can;

(2)  The benefits in a profit-sharing plan reflect a career average formula, rather than a final average formula as often found in a defined benefit plan; and

(3)  Cost can be significantly greater in a defined benefit plan, including the cost of administration.

Due to the complexity involved in the calculations of age-weighted plan, they are not for everyone.  However, there is a time and place for these plans and it is important to know they exist.

# CHAPTER X

*Employee Stock*
*Ownership Plans*
*(ESOPs)*

# Chapter X

## *Employee Stock Ownership Plans (ESOPs)*

An Employee Stock Ownership Plan, or ESOP, is a stock bonus plan, or a stock bonus plan combined with a money purchase pension plan or profit sharing plan, which is designed to invest primarily in the common stock of the employer. Unless there are corporate restrictions on stock holding by non-employees, an ESOP must give a participant the right to require that his distribution upon termination of employment be entirely in the form of employer stock. It must also give him the right to require the employer to purchase any distribution of employer stock made to him if the stock is not readily tradable on an established market.

### Leveraged ESOP

Normally, loans or extensions of credit between an employer and its plan are "prohibited transactions." ERISA makes an exception in the case of ESOPs. Sometimes an ESOP borrows large amounts of money from a financial institution based on the credit (and guarantee) of the employer, then uses the money to purchase the stock of the employer directly from the employer. The employer typically uses the funds to finance major capital purchases. Each year the employer then makes contributions to the ESOP equal to the amount necessary to repay the debt. As the debt is repaid, the stock is allocated to the accounts of the employees. This type if ESOP is called a "leveraged" ESOP.

The complexity of establishing a leveraged ESOP is often not necessary. Similar tax benefits can be achieved if the employer borrows funds directly from a financial institution and contributes an amount of its stock to a stock bonus plan each year equal in value to the amount of its loan repayment.

## Voting Rights

An ESOP must provide that the voting rights of employer stock (with respect to certain major corporate decisions) be passed through to the participants in the plan. This requirement, which applies to approval or disapproval of any corporate merger, recapitalization, liquidation, or similar matter, is not favorable to companies which do not wish to give employees an active voice in the management of the company.

## Investment Options

Although an ESOP is designed to invest primarily in employer stock, participants with at least 10 years of participation, and who have attained age 55, are entitled to diversify a portion of their accounts with general investments. This offers them potential retirement income protection as they reach retirement age. A plan may satisfy the diversification requirement either by offering at least three investment options or by distributing the portion to be diversified. The plan may also permit this portion to be transferred to a defined contribution plan with the same investment options. If the plan makes a distribution, the participant may make a rollover into an IRA.

Further, with respect to stock acquired after 1986, special rules require that, unless a participant elects otherwise, distributions must be made earlier after separation from service and over a shorter period (generally five years) than under the rules applicable to qualified plans in general.

In a closely held company, contributions or sales of stock to an ESOP can significantly dilute the stock ownership over time. This means that the future growth in the value of the company will render in part to the benefit of all of the employees covered under the ESOP, rather than only to the benefit of the original shareholders. However, an ESOP may provide a ready market for the stock of shareholders who have died or retired. This can be a significant advantage for a closely held business. There are special rules, however, regarding sales to the plan by shareholders which prevent any allocation to their accounts or the accounts of any of their relatives for at least ten years.

The Internal Revenue Code contains several favorable provisions relating to the use of ESOPs. There are special rules pertaining to the nonrecognition of gain from selling employer securities to an ESOP when the seller purchases replacement securities. Also, extra contributions made to a leveraged ESOP to repay its loan and certain dividends on stock held by an ESOP, if paid in cash to the participant or used to retire ESOP debt, are deductible by the company.

Corporate lenders, insurance companies, and mutual funds that lend an ESOP money to acquire employer stock may exclude some of the interest income from their gross income if the ESOP owns more than 50% of the stock of the employer after the acquisition. This results in lower interest rates on many ESOP loans.

# CHAPTER XI

*Target Benefit*
*Plans*

# Chapter XI

## *Target Benefit Plans*

Atarget benefit plan is a cross between a money purchase plan and a defined benefit plan. Like a defined benefit plan, a target benefit plan contains a formula which describes a normal retirement benefit for each participant. The employer must then contribute the amount which is estimated as necessary to fund this "targeted" benefit. However, like a money purchase pension plan, contributions to a target benefit plan are allocated to individual accounts for each participant with a maximum annual limit of the lesser of 25% of total compensation or $30,000.

The actual benefit a participant receives at retirement will be based on the value of his account rather than the benefit that was "targeted" under the plan's formula.

For example, the plan may provide that the targeted benefit is 60% of average compensation. Having defined the target benefit, separate accounts are established for each participant and an amount is contributed to each participant's account which (calculated based on a projected rate of future investment earnings known as the level premium funding method) will fund the benefit that is targeted.

The actuarial assumptions of the level premium funding method assume that a particular investment rate of return will be earned on the funds contributed. In the case of a target benefit plan, regardless of the actual fund earnings, the level contribution to the account does not change. Therefore, if the fund's earnings are greater than the actuary has assumed, the participant's actual benefit will be higher than his targeted benefit. On the other hand, if the earnings are lower than the actuarial assumption, the actual benefit will be lower than the targeted benefit.

Since a target benefit plan is set up with a defined benefit formula, it offers similarly favorable results for older employees. Also, since the contributions remain fixed each year, irrespective of investment earnings, the employer exercises cost control. From the participant's perspective, this type of plan is favorable since all investment earnings accumulate in his account rather than being used to reduce the employer's costs.

**Legal Basis**

Target benefit plans are permitted by ERISA, but only in the committee report and in an obsolete provision of the Internal Revenue Code [§410(a)(2)]. Regulations and an important revenue ruling round out the provisions that legalize target benefit plans.

The term "target benefit plan" is no longer part of the Code. At one time, it was described in Code Section 410(a)(2) as one of two types of plans (defined benefit being the other) that could exclude individuals from participation on account of age. That provision was completely rewritten in 1986 eliminating all references to target benefit plans.

Regulations pertaining to that section are still on the books, but are obsolete for all intents and purposes. Those regulations [Section 1.410(a)-4(a)(1)(ii)] contain the following definition:

"For purposes of this paragraph, a target benefit plan is a defined contribution plan under which the amount of employer contributions allocated to each participant is determined under a plan formula which does not allow employer discretion and on the basis of the amount necessary to provide a target benefit specified by the plan for such participant. Such target benefit must be the type of benefit which is provided by a defined benefit plan and the targeted benefit must not discriminate in favor of employees who are officers, shareholders, or highly compensated."

The ERISA committee report for Internal Revenue Code section 415 includes in the definition of defined contribution plans, however, the following statement:

"For purposes of the overall limitations, target benefit plans...are to be treated as defined contribution plans."

The target benefit plan adds an interesting dimension to the retirement plan area. It acts like a defined benefit plan in the beginning, but is treated as a defined contribution plan for administrative purposes. Thus, the age and service advantages for calculating the benefit in a defined benefit plan have been transferred to a defined contribution arena but the baggage attached to defined benefit plans have been left behind: full funding limits, PBGC premiums, actuarial expenses, etc.

While a target benefit plan also enjoys the defined contribution plan advantages, it is not tied down to the one negative that such plans have — a contribution that is based on a level percentage for everyone (assuming non-integrated). The target benefit plan provides better benefits for older employees because of the differing contribution percentages (relative to pay) that a normal defined contribution cannot provide.

Following are some of the key advantages and disadvantages of target benefit plans:

*Advantages:*

- Since a target benefit plan is a defined contribution plan, the annual contribution and deduction is limited to the lesser of 25% of compensation or $30,000 per participant.

- Due to the indirect fixed contribution formula, required contributions can be easily computed and budgeted.

- Favors older employees because there are fewer years during which contributions can be made to arrive at the "anticipated" benefit amounts at retirement.

*Disadvantages:*

- The employer creates a fixed obligation when establishing a target benefit plan and therefore is generally required to contribute the same percentage of compensation or dollar amount selected in year 1 for each subsequent year regardless of profits.

- No in-service distributions are permitted.

- Employer is subject to a 10% underfunding penalty (IRC §4971) if contributions are not made by 8½ months after the end of the employer's tax year and are not made pursuant to the specified contribution formula.

- Contributions in excess of the deductible limit are subject to an excise tax of 10% on any "non-deductible employer contributions" (IRC §4972).

Even though the target benefit plan appears to be complex, it is an extremely attractive type of plan for many employers. Since it is considered by ERISA to be a defined contribution plan, it suffers none of the restrictions placed upon defined benefit plans. However, it also gains the key advantage of defined benefit plans: the ability to vary contributions to the plan according to the age of the individual. Therefore, assuming the same salary, an individual who is age 50 will be credited with a larger contribution than an individual who is 35. This is the principal reason why target benefit plans are useful.

# CHAPTER XII

*Individual
Retirement Accounts
(IRAs)*

# Chapter XII

## *Individual Retirement Accounts (IRAs)*

ection 408 of the Internal Revenue Code defines an Individual Retirement Account as "a trust created or organized in the United States for the exclusive benefit of an individual..." That sounds simple enough, but there are many restrictions and contingencies that apply. The rules can seem very complicated at times so the objective of this chapter is to simplify (as best as possible) the complex.

An IRA is a personal savings plan that enables an individual to set aside money for retirement. The plan is designed for the *Individual.* Joint accounts are not permitted.

In 1974, Congress recognized the need to encourage retirement planning by individuals and passed the Employment Retirement Income Security Act (ERISA). This legislation created the Individual Retirement Account. ERISA initially intended for the IRA to be for individuals not already covered by a company pension plan. However, in 1981 Congress passed the Economic Recovery Tax Act (ERTA) which removed the "active participation" rule and allowed those covered by a company plan to also have an IRA. This Act also increased the contribution limit for IRAs from $1,500 to the current limit of $2,000.

There are two major advantages to having an IRA. First, IRA contributions are generally deductible on an account holder's income tax return. Second, earnings in an IRA are not taxed until they are withdrawn. These "tax-deferred" accrued earnings, over time, can produce large account balances. A person may be in a lower tax bracket at the time of withdrawal.

In order to benefit from an IRA, a person must abide by the rules set by Congress. There are rules regarding eligibility, form, amounts, timing, and deductibility of contributions. There are penalties whenever a person does not follow these rules, and uses the account for purposes other than what Congress intended. . . a Retirement Plan.

## Contributions - Regular IRAs

### *Eligibility*

Nearly anyone who is under the age of 70½ and has "earned income" can contribute to an IRA. No contributions are allowed during the year in which a person reaches the age of 70½, even if still working. A minor can establish an IRA as long as he has earned income.

What is *earned income*? Earned income includes salary, wages, tips, bonuses, professional fees, commissions, and even alimony payments if the alimony in includible in gross income pursuant to a divorce decree. Investment income is not eligible to be used to fund an IRA. Earned income does not include disability payments, pension payments, or income from property owned. For example, if a person does not work but lives on the income from investments, that person does not have earned income and is not eligible to make an IRA contribution.

The account holder must be alive. This may seem obvious at first, but many questions have arisen regarding whether an estate or an individual may make a contribution to a deceased taxpayer's own IRA for the year in which the taxpayer died. In 1984, the IRS issued a *Private Letter Ruling* which stated that a contribution made by an estate to a deceased taxpayer's own IRA would be considered an excess contribution (an excess contribution is subject to a 6% excise tax in the year the contribution was made and for each subsequent year the money remains in the IRA). Even though private letter rulings cannot be relied upon by anyone other that the person requesting the ruling, the 1984 ruling is indicative of the IRS position on the issue.

## *Limitations*

The maximum amount of the contribution is limited to the lesser of 100% of compensation or $2,000 per tax year. If a person has several IRAs, the maximum contribution is the lesser of 100% of compensation or $2,000 to all accounts combined.

A person does not have to make a contribution every year and is not required to contribute the maximum.

## *Timing*

In order for an IRA contribution to qualify for a given tax year, the plan must be established and funded by April 15 of the following year. Therefore, a person actually has 15½ months to make a contribution. Prior to 1984, contributions could be made after April 15 if an individual had a qualified extension to file his tax return. Legislation passed in 1984 did away with this funding privilege. Contributions which are made between January 1 and April 15 for a previous year are called *carryback* contributions. Retroactive contributions are not allowed: A person who did not make a contribution in 1994 cannot make a contribution in 1997 for 1994 (*even if they file an amended return*).

Contributions cannot be made for a future year. A person who has some extra cash in 1997 cannot make a 1998 contribution in 1997.

## *Form*

All contributions to IRAs must be in cash. A person cannot take $2,000 worth of stock personally owned and deposit it into an IRA as a contribution. Most "self-directed" IRAs allow *rollover* contributions in stock or other assets, but a "regular" IRA contribution must be in cash. *Rollover contributions will be discussed in Chapter XVIII.*

## *Documentation*

In order to establish a valid IRA, certain paperwork must be completed. The account holder must receive a disclosure statement and a copy of the plan agreement and sign an acknowledgment (usually an "Adoption Agreement") that he has received these documents. The financial institution's plan must be approved by the IRS. The Plan Agreement is the controlling contract of the IRA. It sets forth the terms and conditions of the IRA, such as contribution limits, investment restrictions, distribution requirements, etc.

An IRA does not exist until the plan agreement is signed by the account holder and accepted by the Trustee or Custodian. The account holder has 7 days from the date of the establishment of the IRA to revoke the IRA.

## Spousal IRAs

The Spousal IRA was created by the Tax Reform Act of 1976. Basically, the plan allows a working, compensated spouse to fund the IRA of a non-working, non-compensated spouse (This is not to be confused with a "Joint IRA"; as mentioned in the Introduction, there is no such thing as a "Joint IRA"). There are certain limitations on contributions and deductions. The benefits, the time frame in which the plan must be established and funded, the form of contributions, and the rules regarding the deductibility of the contributions are the same as a Regular IRA.

To be eligible for a Spousal IRA, the couple must be married and file a joint federal income tax return. One spouse must have earned income and a separate IRA must be established for the non-working, non-compensated spouse. The non-compensated spouse must not have attained the age of 70½. The total contributions to the IRAs cannot exceed the lesser of 100% of the working individual's compensation or $4,000. No more than $2,000 may be put into either IRA.

If a compensated spouse is age 70½ or older and the non-compensated spouse is under the age of 70½, a maximum contribution of $2,000 can be made to the non-compensated spouse's IRA.

A separate account must be established for each person. Both spouses cannot contribute to the same IRA. If the non-employed spouse goes to work and wants to contribute to an IRA, a new IRA does not need to be opened. The spouse who is now employed and has earned income can make contributions based on the "Regular IRA" rules to the existing Spousal IRA.

When Spousal IRAs were first introduced into the law, one spouse must not have had *any* compensation in order to establish a so-called Spousal IRA. Beginning for tax year 1986, either one spouse must not have *any* compensation, (as under prior law), or one spouse may *elect* to be treated as having received no compensation in order to be eligible for a Spousal IRA.

For example, think about the couple where one spouse works and earns $50,000 a year but is over the age of 70½, and the other spouse works and earns only $1,000 a year but is under the age of 70½. This couple still qualifies for "spousal treatment." Although the older spouse may not make a contribution due to age, the younger spouse may elect to be treated as not having earned the $1,000, and a full $2,000 could be contributed into the younger spouse's IRA.

# Deductibility

As stated at the beginning of the chapter, one of the benefits of establishing an IRA is that all or a portion of the contributions may be tax deductible. Prior to the Tax Reform Act of 1986, anyone who made an eligible contribution to an IRA could deduct it from their federal income taxes. However, beginning with IRA contributions for 1987, some account holders now only receive a partial deduction or even no deduction for their IRA contribution. Whether or not a contribution is deductible now depends on whether or not a person is an *"active participant"* in an employer sponsored plan and also on the amount of *"adjusted gross income"* (AGI).

What is an *"active participant?"* A person is an active participant if either the account holder or the account holder's spouse is a participant in an employer-maintained retirement plan such as a qualified pension, profit-sharing, 401(k), or stock bonus plan for any part of the applicable year. Participation in a qualified annuity or Simplified Employee Pension (SEP) would also constitute active participation.

If an individual or spouse is an active participant in a retirement plan, the IRA deduction is phased out when the adjusted gross income (before the IRA contribution) is between $40,000 and $50,000 for joint filers and between $25,000 and $35,000 for single filers.

Adjusted Gross Income (AGI) is determined by adding all sources of income such as salary, wages, interest income, etc., and reducing it by certain "adjustments to income." The IRS has designed a worksheet for the Form 1040 for use in determining what is now know as "Modified Adjusted Gross Income" (MAGI). This basically includes all of the "above the line" adjustments on Form 1040 except for the IRA deduction itself.

Those who are unable to receive a full deduction for their contributions may still choose to make a non-deductible contribution. A non-deductible IRA contribution still has the advantage of tax-deferred earnings. This can result in a significant tax savings over a number of years. An individual does not have to designate a contribution as deductible or non-deductible until the tax return is filed. The individual is not required to report the non-deductible status to the Trustee or Custodian when a contribution is made. Whenever an individual does make a non-deductible contribution, he is required to report it to the IRS on Form 8606 and attach it to the Form 1040. There is a $50 penalty for failure to file the Form 8606.

If an individual takes a distribution from an IRA containing non-deductible contributions, that portion of the distribution representing the non-deductible contribution is not taxable when withdrawn. If an account holder is under the age of 59½ and withdraws a non-deductible contribution, that amount is not subject to the normal 10% premature distribution penalty.

The combined total of deductible and non-deductible contributions cannot exceed the lesser of 100% of compensation or $2,000. Many people think that a non-deductible contribution can be made in excess of the $2,000 limit. This is not true. $2,000 is the limit.

# CHAPTER XIII

*Savings Incentive Match Plans
for Employees
(SIMPLE)*

# Chapter XIII

## *Savings Incentive Match Plan for Employees (SIMPLE)*

The Small Business Job Protection Act was signed into law on August 20, 1996 by President Bill Clinton. The Act created a new simplified retirement plan for small businesses called the Savings Incentive Match Plan for Employees ("SIMPLE" plan), for years beginning after December 31, 1996.

SIMPLE plans can be adopted by employers with 100 or fewer employees. Once an employer with a SIMPLE plan exceeds the 100 employee limit, they can continue to maintain the SIMPLE plan for two years. An employer who maintains a SIMPLE plan is not permitted to maintain another employer-sponsored retirement plan as is allowed with SEPs and SAR-SEPs. Also, employees who received compensation of at least $5,000 from the employer during any two previous years and who are reasonably expected to receive at least that amount during the current year must be eligible to participate. Self-employed individuals are also permitted to participate.

A SIMPLE plan may either be an IRA for each employee or part of a 401(k) plan. If established in IRA form, a SIMPLE plan is not subject to the nondiscrimination rules generally applicable to qualified plans (including top-heavy rules). The employer can either:

1.  Match employee elective contributions dollar-for-dollar up to 3% of compensation (however flexibility is provided by permitting matching contributions of as little as 1% of compensation in no more than two out of five years), or

2.  Choose for any year to make a 2%-of-compensation nonelective contribution for each eligible employee.

*Elective contributions.* A SIMPLE retirement plan allows employees to make elective contributions to the plan. Employee contributions must be expressed as a percentage of the employee's compensation, and can not exceed $6,000 per year (indexed for inflation in $500 increments). Employees can elect to participate or to modify previous contribution elections within 60 days before the start of any year, or 60 days before initial eligibility to participate in the plan. Employees must be allowed to terminate SIMPLE plan participation at any time during the year. SIMPLE plans may permit other changes to salary reduction contributions during the year. Employers must contribute employees' elective deferrals to their accounts within 30 days after the end of the month to which the contributions relate.

*Deductibility.* Employee contributions to a SIMPLE account are fully deductible. Contributions are excludable from the employee's income and are not taxable until withdrawn. Employer contributions generally are deductible if made by the due date (including extensions) of the tax return for the year. Employer matching and nonelective contributions are not considered wages for employment tax and withholding purposes.

*Early withdrawals from SIMPLE accounts.* SIMPLE plan contributions must be fully vested at all times. Early withdrawals from a SIMPLE account are generally subject to the 10% early withdrawal tax applicable to IRAs. However, withdrawals of contributions during the 2-year period beginning on the date the employee first participated in the SIMPLE account are subject to a 25% early withdrawal tax, rather than the 10% tax, to encourage employees to keep money in the SIMPLE account for retirement.

*SIMPLE as part of a 401(k) plan.* Alternatively, a SIMPLE plan can be adopted as part of a 401(k) plan. In that case, the plan does not have to satisfy the special 401(k) nondiscrimination tests for elective deferrals and employer matching contributions, as long as the employer matches elective deferrals made by an employee up to 3% of the employee's compensation, or makes an annual 2%-of-compensation nonelective contribution for eligible employees. In addition, the SIMPLE 401(k) plan is not subject to the top-heavy rules. The other qualified plan rules generally apply, except that there are simplified reporting requirements, and employers and fiduciaries generally have reduced fiduciary liability exposure for losses resulting from the employee or beneficiary exercising control over the assets in his or her account.

**Note:** Employers who establish SIMPLE 401(k) arrangements will not be able to reduce matching contributions to as low as 1% of compensation, as those who maintain SIMPLE IRAs will be permitted to in two out of five years.

# CHAPTER XIV

*General Qualification*
*Rules for Qualified*
*Plans*

# Chapter XIV

## *General Qualification Rules for Qualified Plans*

In order for a plan to be considered a "qualified plan," it must meet certain specified tax rules. These rules are called "plan qualification rules." Here, in digest form, are the main general qualification rules:

**Rule 1.** The plan must be a definite written program setting forth all provisions essential for qualification. If the plan utilizes a trust, there must be a written trust instrument.

**Rule 2.** The plan must be communicated to employees.

**Rule 3.** The plan must be established by the employer.

**Rule 4.** The plan must be permanent.

**Rule 5.** The plan must be for the exclusive benefit of employees or their beneficiaries. Benefits provided for beneficiaries must be incidental to those provided for employees.

**Rule 6.** Contributions or benefits provided under the plan must not discriminate in favor of highly compensated employees.

**Rule 7.** The plan must satisfy a set of minimum vesting standards.

**Rule 8.** The plan must satisfy minimum participation and coverage requirements.

**Rule 9.** It must be impossible under the plan for any part of the plan's assets to be used for, or diverted to, purposes other than for the exclusive benefit of the employees or their beneficiaries.

**Rule 10.** A defined benefit plan, a money purchase plan, and in some cases, a profit sharing plan must provide automatic survivor benefits in the form of a qualified joint and survivor annuity and a qualified pre-retirement survivor annuity.

**Rule 11.** The plan must not provide contributions and benefits for individual employees that exceed certain limitations.

**Rule 12.** The plan may not require that an employee forfeit any part of his accrued benefit derived from employer contributions solely because of his withdrawal of any part of the benefits derived from his own contributions.

**Rule 13.** The plan must provide that, unless the participant elects otherwise, payment of benefits must begin not later than 60 days after the close of the plan year in which the latest occurs: (a) the participant attains age 65 or earlier normal retirement age; (b) the tenth anniversary of the time when the participant began participation in the plan; or (c) the participant terminates service with the employer.

| | |
|---|---|
| **Rule 14.** | The plan must provide that a participant's benefits will not be reduced because of changes in social security wage benefits or wage base. |
| **Rule 15.** | The plan must provide for both before-death and after-death required distribution rules. |
| **Rule 16.** | The plan must provide that all participants will become vested in the event of plan termination. |
| **Rule 17.** | The plan must provide that in the case of any merger or transfer of assets from one plan to another, each participant will receive a benefit immediately after the merger, etc. which is not less than the value of the benefit he would have been entitled to receive immediately before the merger, etc. |
| **Rule 18.** | The plan must provide that benefits under the plan may not be assigned or alienated. |
| **Rule 19.** | A terminating pension plan may provide for a qualified total distribution without disqualifying the plan. |
| **Rule 20.** | A defined benefit plan, whenever the amount of any benefit is determined on the basis of actuarial assumptions, must specify such assumptions in the plan in a way which precludes employer discretion. |
| **Rule 21.** | A defined benefit plan may not allocate forfeitures among remaining participants to increase their benefits. |
| **Rule 22.** | A plan must provide that only the first $150,000 (indexed for inflation, beginning in 1994) of an |

employee's compensation may be taken into account in determining contributions or benefits under the plan.

**Rule 23.**   A plan must benefit no fewer than the lesser of: (a) 50 employees, or (b) 40 percent or more of all employees of the employer.

**Rule 24.**   A plan which is intended to be a money purchase plan or a profit-sharing plan must designate its intention at such time and in such manner as is prescribed by the IRS.

Please keep in mind that this is an extremely simplified listing of the qualification rules. Should you desire further research, a good place to start would be Section 401(a) of the Internal Revenue Code.

# CHAPTER XV

*Eligibility Requirements*

# Chapter XV

## *Eligibility Requirements*

The eligibility requirements differ substantially from plan to plan. For example, the minimum age and service conditions stated in Internal Revenue Code Section 410(a)(1) require that an employee be eligible to participate in a *qualified plan* no later than:

(i) the date on which the employee attains the age of 21, or
(ii) the date on which he completes one year of service.

However, the rules found in Internal Revenue Code Section 408(k)(2) require than an employee be eligible to participate in a *simplified employee pension (SEP) plan* no later than:

(A) the year in which the employee attains the age of 21, or
(B) the time in which the employee has performed service for the employer during at least 3 of the immediately preceding 5 years, and received at least $300 in compensation ($400 for 1997 due to cost of living adjustments) from the employer for the year.

Obviously, two very similar but very different sets of rules for the type main types of employer sponsored plans. On the following page is a chart that breaks down the eligibility requirements (in its simplest form) to help with an understanding of the differences:

| Eligibility Requirements | |
|---|---|
| **IRA** | Anyone with earned income and under the age of 70½ |
| **SEP** | May be less, but cannot exclude those who have attained:<br>• 21 years of age<br>• Employed 3 of the last 5 years<br>• $300 annual income†<br>Requires 100% participation of all eligible employees. |
| **SAR-SEP** | May be less, but cannot exclude those who have achieved:<br>• 21 years of age<br>• Employed 3 of the last 5 years<br>• $300 annual income*<br>Requires 50% participation of all eligible employees. Employer may not have more than 25 eligible employees. |
| **Profit-Sharing, Money Purchase & Defined Benefit** | May be less, but cannot exclude those who have reached:<br>• 21 years of age<br>• Completion of one year of service. (May be 2 years of service if vesting is 100% full and immediate)<br>• 1000 hours of service per year. |
| **401(k)** | May be less, but cannot exclude those who have attained:<br>• 21 years of age<br>• Completion of one year of service.<br>• 1000 hours of service per year. |

---

* For 1997, the minimum compensation for exclusionary purposes is $400 due to COLA increases.

# CHAPTER XVI

*Definitions of*
*Compensation*

# Chapter XVI

## *Definitions of Compensation*

G enerally, basic *compensation* means the compensation received by the employee for services performed for the employer for the "applicable period" that is currently included in gross income for tax purposes [IRS Temp. Reg. 1.414(s)-1T, Q&A 1(a)].

This definition can be found in the Internal Revenue Code under §414(s) and applies to all sections of the Code that specifically cross reference §414(s). However, this definition does not apply where a Code section has its own definition of compensation. For example, Limitations on Contributions found under §415 of the Code contains its own definition of compensation, therefore the §414(s) definition does not apply.

(Now all of these §s and ( )s and Codes, etc. probably make you want to say #&@! But please bear with me through these next couple of paragraphs):

An employer may use any definition of compensation that satisfies Section 414(s) to determine if an applicable provision is satisfied with respect to a qualified retirement plan. This rule is designed to permit an employer, whenever possible, to use the definition used under the plan for calculating contributions or benefits to determine if an applicable nondiscrimination provision is satisfied. Consequently, an employer that maintains more than one qualified plan may generally use one definition of compensation that satisfies

131

Section 414(s) in determining whether one of the plans satisfies a particular nondiscrimination requirement and use the same or a different definition of compensation in determining whether another plan satisfies the same nondiscrimination requirement.

The definition of compensation selected generally must be used consistently to define the compensation of all employees taken into account in determining whether a plan satisfies the nondiscrimination provision.

A definition of compensation that includes all compensation within the meaning of Section 415(c)(3) and excludes all other compensation will automatically satisfy Section 414(s).

Section 415(c)(3) is reproduced below:

> 415(c)(3) PARTICIPANT'S COMPENSATION.--For purposes of paragraph (1)--
>
> 415(c)(3)(A) IN GENERAL.--The term "participant's compensation" means the compensation of the participant from the employer for the year.
>
> 415(c)(3)(B) SPECIAL RULE FOR SELF-EMPLOYED INDIVIDUALS.--In the case of an employee within the meaning of section 401(c)(1), subparagraph (A) shall be applied by substituting "the participant's earned income (within the meaning of section 401(c)(2) but determined without regard to any exclusion under section 911)" for "compensation of the participant from the employer."

**Determining "Compensation" for Self-Employed Individuals**

"Compensation" for a self-employed individual (sole proprietor or partner) is that person's *earned income,* **not** net profit. Earned income is a derivative of net profit, therefore the first step is to determine the self-employed person's net profit amount from the Schedule C (or Schedule K-1 in the case of a partnership).

Since a self-employed individual deducts a plan contribution for his own behalf and also deducts ½ of the self-employment taxes (SET) in the "Adjustments to Income" section of their personal income tax return (Form 1040), these amounts must also be taken into consideration in determining the "earned income" amount. Therefore, the earned income formula looks like this:

**Earned Income = Net Profit - the Contribution - ½ SET**

Now, anyone familiar with algebra may recognize what seems to be a problem with the above equation: Before we can calculate the *contribution*, we must calculate the *earned income*...but we can't calculate the *earned income* without knowing what *contribution* amount to plug in!

Stay with me, there's a relatively easy solution to this and its called the *equivalency method*. Whenever the plan calls for a certain percentage of "earned income" to be contributed on behalf of a self-employed individual, the *equivalency method* computes an *equivalent percentage* to be used with "adjusted net profit." To determine the "adjusted net profit", the net profit (from Schedule C) is simply reduced by the ½ Self-Employment Tax (from Schedule SE).

The equivalency percentages are determined by dividing the desired plan percentage by "1.the" percentage (as an example, consider: 15% ÷ 1.15 = 13.04348%). The equivalency percentage multiplied by adjusted net profit will equal exactly the true percentage multiplied by earned income. *Note:* This method may *only* be used if the person has just *one plan*.

The following chart will provide a quick reference to the equivalency percentages. The last two digits of the equivalency percentages have been omitted:

# Earned Income Equivalency Chart for Self-Employed Individuals

| % of earned income | = | % of adjusted net profit |
|:---:|:---:|:---:|
| 25%................................................. | | ...20.000% |
| 24%................................................. | | ...19.355% |
| 23%................................................. | | ...18.699% |
| 22%................................................. | | ...18.033% |
| 21%................................................. | | ...17.355% |
| 20%................................................. | | ...16.667% |
| 19%................................................. | | ...15.966% |
| 18%................................................. | | ...15.254% |
| 17%................................................. | | ...14.530% |
| 16%................................................. | | ...13.793% |
| **15%.................................................** | | **...13.043%** |
| 14%................................................. | | ...12.281% |
| 13%................................................. | | ...11.504% |
| 12%................................................. | | ...10.714% |
| 11%................................................. | | ...9.910% |
| 10%................................................. | | ...9.091% |
| 9%................................................. | | ...8.257% |
| 8%................................................. | | ...7.407% |
| 7%................................................. | | ...6.542% |
| 6%................................................. | | ...5.660% |
| 5%................................................. | | ...4.762% |
| 4%................................................. | | ...3.846% |
| 3%................................................. | | ...2.913% |
| 2%................................................. | | ...1.961% |
| 1%................................................. | | ...0.990% |

*Please Note:* As a result of final regulations under §414(s) of the Internal Revenue Code, the definition of compensation on behalf of self-employed individuals must be the language of the Code §415 safe harbor definition of compensation. Because the actual definition of compensation is extremely complicated and can vary from plan to plan, it is important that you consult your tax advisor before proceeding with any particular definition in your plan. [A good source for detailed information on the definitions of compensation can be found in *Qualified Plans - Above and Beyond,* published by PenServ, Inc. They can be reached at (903) 455-5135.]

# CHAPTER XVII

*Contributions*
*& Deductions*

# Chapter XVII

## *Contributions & Deductions*

Throughout this book, we have talked about the different types of employer sponsored retirement plans and how they can benefit the small business. One of the greatest benefits to the employer is indicated in the title of this book: *100% Deductible.* Virtually all of the retirement plan types described in this book allow the employer to deduct from taxation 100% of the amount contributed to the plan. There are limits however to the amounts that may be contributed. Following is a brief explanation of the contribution limits as they apply to the various types of plans:

### *Profit Sharing Plan*

The maximum annual deductible contribution to a profit sharing plan by an employer is limited to the lesser of 15% of total compensation or $30,000. (Keep in mind, also, that there is also a maximum amount of compensation that may be considered in determining the contribution. This will be discussed in more detail later in this chapter.)

Profit sharing plans also allow the employer flexibility in determining the contribution amount each year. The plan's allocation formula may be altered by the employer from year to year. In one year the employer may decide to contribute 15% of compensation to the plan, and the next year he may decide that only 10% will be contributed...or 5%...or 2%.

An employer could decide to not even make a contribution for a particular year or years. However, making a single or occasional contribution out of profits does not establish a plan of profit sharing. The IRS regulations state that profit sharing contributions must be made on a "substantial and recurring basis" in order to be considered to be a tax qualified plan. If the employer fails to make such substantial and recurring profit sharing contributions, the employer may risk the plan being deemed terminated by the IRS. When a deemed termination occurs, the assets of the plan must be distributed to the participants and are taxable at that time.

The regulations provide that a qualified plan must be established with the intent of maintaining an ongoing, permanent program. Although the employer may reserve the right to change or terminate the plan, or discontinue the contributions thereunder, the abandonment of the plan for any reason other than business necessity within a few years after it has been established will be evidence that the plan *from its inception* was **not** a bona fide qualified plan.

The Code permits an employer to make discretionary profit sharing plan contributions, even if the business does not have any net profits. However, if the business is unincorporated, profit sharing contributions may be made on behalf of the self-employed individual(s) *only* if the business has net profits.

### Money Purchase Pension Plans

Unlike profit sharing plans, an employer who establishes a money purchase pension plan is *required* to make a contribution each and every year as specified in the plan's adoption agreement.

The maximum annual contribution which may be specified in the plan's adoption agreement is the lesser of 25% of total compensation or $30,000 per participant. In a money purchase pension plan, the employer has no discretion in making contributions each year. Money purchase pension plans are in no way geared to the profits of the employer. Employer contributions must be made on behalf of regular eligible employees as specified in the plan document and adoption agreement regardless of profits.

### Simplified Employee Pension (SEP) Plans

Contributions under a SEP are limited each year to the lesser of 15% of *each* employee's compensation or $30,000. In addition, employer contributions under a SEP must bear a uniform relationship to the compensation of each employee covered under the SEP plan. In other words, if the business owner contributes 15% of his own compensation, each eligible employee must also receive a contribution of 15% of their compensation (without regard to Social Security Integration).

An employer has total flexibility in determining the percentage of compensation to contribute to the plan from year to year. There is no "substantial and recurring" rule for SEPs as there is for profit sharing plans (see *Profit Sharing Plans* at the beginning of this chapter). The only requirement placed upon the employer is that the employer must disclose *in writing* each year to each eligible employee the "allocation formula."

### Maximum Compensation Considered

Whether the employer is contributing to a profit sharing plan, a money purchase pension plan, or a simplified employee pension (SEP) plan, the maximum compensation which may be considered in determining the employer contribution is limited to $160,000 (1997 figure; subject to cost of living adjustments) for each employee.

From 1989 to 1994, the maximum compensation limit was $200,000 and indexed upward for cost of living adjustments. However, as a result of the Omnibus Budget Reconciliation Act of 1993 (OBRA '93), Congress reduced the maximum compensation limit beginning with 1994 to $150,000. This compensation limit is also subject to cost of living adjustments but only in increments of $10,000 rounded down to the next lowest increment of $10,000. Therefore, the limit of $150,000 has remained unchanged until 1997.

Following is a table of the compensation limits as adjusted for the cost of living since 1989:

| Year | Limit |
|------|-------|
| 1989 | $200,000 |
| 1990 | $209,200 |
| 1991 | $222,220 |
| 1992 | $228,860 |
| 1993 | $235,840 |
| 1994 | $150,000 |
| 1995 | $150,000 |
| 1996 | $150,000 |
| 1997 | $160,000 |

For plan years that are not calendar years, the applicable compensation limit is the limit for the calendar year in which the fiscal years begins.

# CHAPTER XVIII

*Rollovers*
*& Transfers*

# Chapter XVIII

## *Rollovers & Transfers*

### Direct Rollovers

As a result of former President George Bush signing the *Unemployment Compensation Amendments Act of 1992*, beginning January 1, 1993 a qualified plan participant **must** be given the option to elect to have his eligible rollover distribution made in a *direct rollover* payment to the trustee/custodian of an eligible retirement plan.

For purposes of these rules, an eligible retirement plan includes an IRA or another defined contribution qualified plan which accepts rollover contributions. *If an employer fails to permit such an election to his employees, the employer's plan incurs the risk of being disqualified!*

If a participant does not elect to have the eligible rollover distribution paid in a Direct Rollover to another plan, the employer is required to withhold federal income tax at a rate of 20%. The participant may **not** waive this withholding requirement.

In other words, if the participant requests that the employer actually distribute the amount to him, 20% must be withheld from the payment as a prepayment of the income tax liability due on the amount of the eligible rollover distribution.

The individual would be able to claim the amount withheld as a payment of taxes when the income tax return is filed and may be entitled to a refund, depending on the individual's total tax liability for the year. However, because this distribution is still eligible to be rolled over to another plan within 60 days of receipt and avoid current taxation, the individual would have to come up with additional funds in order to rollover the entire taxable amount.

If an employee elects to have a portion of an eligible rollover distribution paid as a Direct Rollover to another plan and to receive the remainder as a distribution, the 20% mandatory withholding only applies to the portion of the distribution actually received by the individual and not the portion paid as a direct rollover.

*IRA distributions are not subject to the 20% withholding requirement (Reg. Section 31.3405(c)-1T).*

The mandatory 20% withholding applicable to eligible rollover distributions from employer sponsored plans **does not apply** to IRA distributions. All IRA distributions are governed by the previous and existing rules. This means that withholding will apply to any IRA distribution at the rate of 10%, unless the payee is eligible for and elects for no withholding to apply.

## Trustee-to-Trustee Transfers

A trustee-to-trustee transfer is a direct transfer of assets between retirement plan trusts and is neither a taxable distribution nor a rollover. *Throughout this chapter, whenever I refer to "trustee" or "trust", it shall include "custodian" and "custodial account," respectively.* There is actually no Internal Revenue Code provision permitting these direct transfers. Rather, they were created by the IRS's administrative revenue ruling program and defined further only in private letter rulings to individual taxpayers. These

144

rulings are based on the principle that there is neither actual nor constructive receipt of income where retirement plan assets are transferred directly between plans by the plan trustee without ever being subject to the disposal of the plan participant (This all made perfectly good sense until we got the "direct *rollover*", but let's not confuse the issue).

Since these transfers go directly from one trust to another, the IRS has held that these transfers do not constitute a distribution. Therefore, this type of transaction is not reported to the IRS by the trustee. This type of transaction is not taxable to the account holder nor is withholding required. The IRS has imposed no limits on how often a transfer can be made. A transfer may be full or partial.

A trustee-to-trustee transfer may only be made between "like" plans. For example, between an IRA and an IRA; or between a qualified plan and another qualified plan. A transfer between an IRA and a qualified plan, such as a profit sharing plan, is not permitted (again, not to be confused with a direct rollover, which is a reportable event).

# CHAPTER XIX

*General Distribution*
*Rules*

# Chapter XIX

## *General Distribution Rules*

Under the Internal Revenue Code, as amended by ERISA, a qualified plan must include certain provisions regarding the time that benefits will be distributed from the plan (see Chapter XIV, rule numbers 13, 14, and 15). The plan must permit that a participant's benefit will be paid to him, unless he "elects otherwise," no later than 60 days after the end of the plan year in which the *latest* of the following occurs:

(i)     The date on which he attains age 65 (or the plan's normal retirement age, if earlier);

(ii)    The tenth anniversary of the year in which he commenced participation in the plan; **or**

(iii)   The date on which he terminates service with the employer.

There is a rule in tax law known as the "doctrine of constructive receipt." This rules works to include in a person's taxable income money that is available to him, even if he decides not to receive it (*Treasury Regulation §1.451-2*).

### *Premature Distributions*

In general, all qualified plan participants are subject to a 10% additional income tax if a taxable distribution is made prior to the participant attaining age 59½. However, there are a few exceptions to this rule. The following distributions are not subject to the premature distribution penalty:

1. taxable distributions received on or after the date the participant attains the age of 59½;

2. taxable distributions due to death;

3. taxable distributions due to the participant becoming disabled;

4. if the participant has separated from service, a distribution of substantially equal periodic payments, not less frequent than annual, over the life or life expectancy of the participant, or over the joint life or joint life expectancies of the participant and the designated beneficiary;

5. a distribution to a participant who has separated from service *and* has attained the age of 55; **or**

6. taxable distributions made to an alternate payee under a qualified domestic relations order (QDRO).

There are a few other exception listed in Section 72(t) of the Internal Revenue Code which are a little more complicated. Should the situation arise, you should definitely consult a tax advisor before taking any action.

### *In-Service Distributions*

In-service distributions are distributions which are made to participants while they are still employed by the employer. These types of distributions are not permitted under "pension" plans (i.e., money purchase, target benefit, defined benefit plans). Many profit sharing and 401(k) plans do, however, allow for in-service distributions. There are three basic in-service distribution provisions which may be used. They are as follows:

1.  **24 month rule.** A participant may withdraw any contribution (but no earnings attributable) which has been in the plan for a period of 24 months.

2.  **60 month rule.** Once a participant has been in the plan for 60 months, he may withdraw any or all vested contributions, plus earnings.

3.  **Hardship Distributions.** The plan document will specify what criteria must be met in order for a hardship withdrawal to be permitted. Normally, there must be an immediate financial need to qualify for hardship distributions. Hardship withdrawals could include medical expenses which are deductible on the participant's federal income tax return; illness or disability which prevent the participant from gainful employment for a specified period of time; the threatened bankruptcy of the participant or the foreclosure of a mortgage on the participant's principal residence; the education of the participant's children; or the purchase of the participant's primary residence.

### Survivor Annuity Distribution Requirements

In general, all pension plans (not including SEPs) must comply with the Joint and Survivor Annuity and the Pre-retirement Annuity requirements for all participants who are credited with one hour of service.

Generally, a qualified plan must provide an automatic annuity to the surviving spouse of a participant who does not die before the "annuity starting date" under a joint and survivor annuity or to a surviving spouse of a vested participant who dies before the "annuity starting date" under a pre-retirement survivor annuity.

In order to elect out of the joint and survivor annuity and pre-retirement annuity coverage, written spousal consent is required. In addition, the employer is required to provide written explanations of both the pre-retirement survivor annuity and the joint and survivor annuity to the participant and spouse at specified times.

*Qualified Joint and Survivor Annuity:*

A qualified joint and survivor annuity (QJSA) is an annuity for the life of the participant with a survivor annuity for the life of the spouse that is not less than 50% or more than 100% of the amount that is payable during the joint lives of the participant and spouse. In the case of an unmarried participant, the normal form of benefit is a single life annuity. An unmarried participant may waive the annuity requirement by simply selecting another form of payment on the trustee's distribution form.

A qualified plan is required to provide for a participant to receive a QJSA when he attains the earliest retirement age under the plan.

*Qualified Pre-retirement Survivor Annuity:*

A qualified pre-retirement survivor annuity (QPSA) is an annuity for the life of the surviving spouse of the participant.

Under a defined contribution plan, the payments under a QPSA are not to be less than payments under a single life annuity, the present value of which is at least equal to 50% of the participant's vested account balance on the participant's date of death.

# CHAPTER XX

*Required Distributions*
*at Age 70½*

# Chapter XX

## *Required Distributions at Age 70½*

When a qualified plan participant reaches the age of 70½, he is subject to a *Required Minimum Distribution*. When Congress created qualified plans, it was their intention to encourage retirement planning through tax-deferred savings. They never intended for these plans to be used to permanently shelter these dollars from taxation. Therefore, participants who are age 70½ or older must take mandatory distributions. Failure to withdraw the required minimum could subject the participant to a *50% penalty tax* (yes *50%*, this is not a "typo") on the amount that should have been withdrawn.

The first distribution can be delayed until April 1st of the year following the year in which the participant attains the age of 70½. Only the first distribution may be delayed. Subsequent distributions must be withdrawn by December 31st of each year.

The amount that must be withdrawn is based on life expectancy. If the participant's primary beneficiary is his spouse, then the minimum distribution is determined by using the *joint* life expectancy tables developed by the IRS (If the primary beneficiary is someone other than, or in addition to, the participant's spouse, the same joint life expectancy tables may be used, **but** the beneficiary cannot be treated as being more than 10 years younger than the participant).

The Required Minimum Distribution (RMD) is calculated by dividing the value of the account on December 31st of the year preceding the year the account holder actually turns 70½ by the life expectancy "factor." For example: If a participant turned 70 on January 30, 1997, he would be age 70½ on August 31, 1997. The participant would then have until April 1, 1998 to take the required minimum distribution. If the value of the account on December 31, 1996 was $200,000, the RMD would by $12,500 (the *factor* for a participant age 70 is *16*; Thus, $200,000 divided by 16 equals $12,500). The second RMD would have to be withdrawn by December 31, 1998.

* Effective for years beginning after 1996, the requirement that all qualified plan participants who remain employed begin receiving distributions by age 70½ has been replaced with a requirement that distributions begin by April 1 of the calendar year following the later of the calendar year in which the employee reaches age 70½ or the calendar year in which the employee retires. A special rule applies to employees who are 5% owners or IRA holders, and an actuarial adjustment rule may apply to them, also.

# CHAPTER XXI

*Required Distributions*
*at Death*

# Chapter XXI

## *Required Distributions at Death*

There are generally two sets of rules to follow in determining how to withdraw qualified retirement funds upon the death of a participant. The rules vary depending on when the participant's death occurs relative to his attaining the age of 70½. Following are the general rules for the beneficiary of a deceased qualified plan participant:

**Where the participant dies *on or after* his "required beginning date" (April 1st following the calendar year in which the participant attains the age of 70½):**

For deaths occurring on or after an individual's required beginning date, there is just one rule to remember: The remaining portion of the beneficiary's interest in the plan must be distributed at least as rapidly as the method of distributions being used by the participant before death. The beneficiary can always accelerate payments; even a complete distribution could be made. (In some cases, "at least as rapidly" means "more rapid", depending on the life expectancies of the parties involved.)

**Where the IRA owner dies *before* his Required Beginning Date:**

*The 5-Year Rule*

The general rule says that the entire portion of the beneficiary's interest must be distributed no later than December 31st of the calendar year containing the *fifth* anniversary of the participant's death.

## The Exception to the 5-Year Rule

The exception to the general rule says that, if beginning no later than December 31st of the calendar year following the year of the participant's death, the portion of the beneficiary's interest may begin to be distributed to such beneficiary over the beneficiary's life or over the single life expectancy of the *"designated"* beneficiary. In order for this exception to apply, the plan must have a "designated beneficiary." NOTE: This is the only exception to the 5-Year rule available to a non-spouse beneficiary.

## Special Rule for Surviving Spouse Beneficiary

A special rule exists where the surviving spouse is the *sole* designated beneficiary which says that the earliest date death distributions are required to commence is December 31st of the calendar year in which the deceased participant would have attained the age of 70½ had he lived, if later than the one year period.

A spouse beneficiary also has the option of taking a distribution from the decedent's plan and rolling over that distribution to his or her own IRA. This option is not available to a non-spouse beneficiary.

## DEFINITIONS:

### Designated Beneficiary:

In order for the exception to the 5-Year Rule to apply, the participant account must have a "designated beneficiary." Only an individual may be a designated beneficiary. If another entity, such as an individual's estate, charity, etc. is named as primary beneficiary, even though another individual is also named, the participant's account will be deemed not to have a designated beneficiary.

## *Exception in the Case of a Trust Named as Beneficiary*

As in the case of determining the designated beneficiary when a participant reaches the age of 70½, the beneficiaries of a trust which meets the following requirements may be used to determine the exception to the 5-Year Rule:

1.  The trust is a valid trust under state law, or would be but for the fact that there is no corpus;

2.  The trust is irrevocable;

3.  The beneficiaries of the trust are identifiable from the trust instrument;

**AND**

4.  A copy of the trust instrument is provided to the plan.

## *Multiple Primary Beneficiaries*

For purposes of determining the distribution period under the exception to the 5-Year Rule, the life expectancy factor of the designated beneficiary with the shortest life expectancy (determined as of the participant's death) will be used to calculate the required death distributions to all individual beneficiaries.

# CHAPTER XXII

*Vesting Rules*

# Chapter XXII

## *Vesting Rules*

The terms of the plan dictate how much of a participant's account balance will be available to him if he terminates employment prior to retirement. All plans must adopt a vesting schedule permitted under ERISA which gives each participant a nonforfeitable right to a certain percentage of his account balance depending on his years of service with the company. As an example, a typical vesting schedule may provide that a participant will be vested in 20% of his account balance each year so that at the end of five years he is 100% vested in the entire account balance. This type of vesting schedule is generally referred to as a *graded vesting schedule.*

Some companies use a graded vesting schedule while others provide 100 percent vesting at *x* years of service with no vesting prior to that (called "cliff" vesting). Plans that are deemed "top heavy" (plans that primarily benefit the top employees) must utilize a vesting schedule which gives a participant at least 20% vesting after two years of service and an additional 20% each year thereafter until the participant is 100% vested when he has six years of service. These are statutory minimums, a plan sponsor may always be *less* restrictive. No matter what type of vesting schedule is adopted, though, it must not discriminate in favor of the highly compensated employees.

A participant is always 100% vested in the account balance for his own contributions to the plan. Also, participants in a SEP or SIMPLE plan are always 100% vested.

## Forfeitures

If an employee terminates employment before becoming 100 percent vested in his account balance, the unvested portion is forfeited. Usually the forfeitures are allocated among the remaining participants in exactly the same manner as the employer contribution by using the ratio that each participant's compensation bears to the total compensation of all participants for the plan year in which the forfeiture occurs.

The forfeiture amounts may either be allocated as provided above or may be used by the employer to offset contribution amounts for the future year.

# CHAPTER XXIII

*Prohibited*
*Transactions*

# Chapter XXIII

## *Prohibited Transactions*

Section 4975 of the Internal Revenue Code deals with *Prohibited Transactions.* Basically, prohibited transactions include sales, purchases, leases, and loans between a plan and a "disqualified person." The term "disqualified person" *generally* means a person who is: (1) a fiduciary; (2) a person providing services to the plan; (3) an employer who has any employees covered by the plan; (4) an employee organization any of whose members are covered by the plan; (5) an owner, direct or indirect, of 50% of the combined voting power of all classes of stock of a corporation; (6) A family member of any individual described in the previous definitions; or (7) an officer, director, or 10% or more shareholder of a person described above.

Individuals who establish self-directed retirement plans and direct their accounts into companies that they own engage in a prohibited act of self-dealing, since they become fiduciaries of the accounts. Prohibited transactions also include transactions between the plan and a member of the account holder's family; or between the plan and entities (corporations, partnerships) in which the account holder may have a controlling interest (more than 50%). Any transaction between an plan and a corporation of which the account holder is an officer could also be deemed a prohibited transaction.

Loans from an Individual Retirement Account (IRA) are not permitted. To pledge or assign an IRA as security for a loan is also a prohibited transaction. Since this type of transaction benefits the "individual" and not the "Plan," Congress has disallowed it based on the premise that it does not conform with the intended purpose of an IRA . . . to provide for *retirement*. However, certain qualified plans, such as Profit Sharing and 401(k) plans do allow for loan provisions.

The Code strictly disallows an individual to invest retirement plan funds in "collectibles," such as antiques, rugs, stamps, gems, coins, or any other tangible personal property. Prior to 1982, retirement plans could invest in such items, so collectibles may be included in a plan established and invested before this date. Another exception to this rule: The Tax Reform Act of 1986 modified the rules on collectibles to permit plan participants to invest in the United States gold and silver coins commonly known as American Eagle coins. The Technical and Miscellaneous Act of 1988 (TAMRA) extended this exception to also include any state issued coins. IRA funds may not be used to purchase life insurance contracts, however, many qualified plans are allowed to do so.

***An IRA ceases to be an IRA if an account holder engages in a prohibited transaction.*** The account holder is deemed to have received the entire fair market value of the IRA as of the first day of the year in which the prohibited transaction occurred. If an account is disqualified as such, the value of the account is treated as a taxable distribution and must be included in the individual's gross income (including any excess or non-deductible contributions which could have otherwise been returned tax-free). Furthermore, if the individual has not attained the age of 59½, the distribution is subject to the 10% additional premature distribution tax.

For a qualified plan, a penalty of 5% on the amounts involved in the prohibited transaction will be assessed against the disqualified person responsible for the prohibited transaction. If the transaction is not corrected during the "taxable period"

170

then a 100% (yes, this is not a misprint - 100%) penalty of the amount involved is assessed against the disqualified person.

Generally, with a few exceptions, permissible investments include the same form of investments allowed in any other brokerage account. These typically include marketable securities traded on a recognized exchange or "over-the-counter." Permissible investments also include certificates of deposit, mutual funds, money market funds, covered call options, government securities, certain unit investment trusts, and certain annuity contracts.

It is important to be familiar with the prohibited transaction rules when dealing with a self-directed account. While a particular investment may appear to provide a great return, in order to be invested in a qualified plan, it must meet the requirements set by Congress.

# CHAPTER XXIV

*Responsibilities of the Parties under the Plan*

# Chapter XXIV

## *Responsibilities of the Parties under the Plan*

It is important to understand before adopting a qualified plan who the parties involved with the plan are and in general terms what their responsibilities are with respect to the operation and administration of the qualified plan. The following is a brief description of the various parties under the plan, the purpose of each, and the responsibilities associated with each:

### The Sponsoring Organization

Generally, the sponsoring organization (not to be confused with the term "Plan Sponsor" who is generally the employer) is the entity which "sponsors" the plan by writing and submitting the plan to the IRS, and assures the qualified status of the plan for the employer. The IRS limits the types of organizations that are eligible to sponsor Master or Prototype Plans. Sponsoring organizations are limited to:

- Banks;
- Credit Unions;
- Insurance companies;
- Regulated investment companies (mutual funds);
- Investment Advisors that have an advisory contract with one or more regulated investment companies;
- IRS-approved non-bank trustees;
- Trade or professional organizations.

The sponsoring organization must furnish all adopting employers with copies of all IRS National Office Opinion Letters, including those covering any amendments.

### *The Depository*

The depository merely accepts deposits and has no fiduciary responsibilities. The institution or firm that offers the Plan may wish to serve merely as depository with respect to some employer's plans and Trustee or Custodian (see below) with respect to others.

### *The Trustee (or Custodian)*

The trustee serves in a fiduciary capacity and does all the accounting functions. The trustee is required to keep separate accounts or separate accounting for each employee. The trustee is accountable for all contributions delivered to it, but is not responsible to determine whether the contributions are in the correct amounts.

Unlike IRAs, the trustee or custodian of a qualified plan need not be a "bank". Any "person" who is eligible to be a trustee under the laws of the state in which the trust is established may serve in that capacity. It is not uncommon in the case of small plans for the owner(s) of the business to serve as trustee.

### *The Employer*

The employer is the corporation or unincorporated business adopting the plan (sometimes call the Plan Sponsor). Under many plans, unless the employer designates a plan administrator, the employer itself shall also assume the responsibilities listed below.

## *The Plan Administrator*

The plan administrator is the person or firm designated by the employer to be responsible for all reporting and disclosure pursuant to Title I of ERISA. The plan administrator is responsible for income tax withholding on distributions unless delegated to a payor.

Under many plans, if no plan administrator is named, the employer automatically becomes the plan administrator.

The plan administrator has the responsibility for overall administration on a day-to-day basis and control of the plan.

# CHAPTER XXV

*Final Comments*

# Chapter XXV

## *Final Comments*

Qualified plans provide your company with tax deductions and help you and your employees accumulate capital. Choosing the plan that's best for your organization depends on proper analysis and a clear understanding of your objectives. Whichever qualified plan you choose, they all have important advantages for you — the employer.

♦ They enhance your competitive position in the labor marketplace.

♦ They provide you and your employees with logical, effective ways to accumulate capital and retirement income.

♦ They provide you with tax deductions for your plan contributions and administrative expenses.

♦ Profit sharing plans and 401(k) plans motivate employees to take a more personal interest in the company's success.

♦ Employee stock ownership plans can increase cash flow and working capital, can create a market for closely held stock, and can provide cash for current stockholders.

The amount of capital you can accumulate over a 30 year period with a qualified plan is astounding. For example: If you start a money purchase pension plan and a 401(k) plan now...with combined annual funding to your accounts in those plans of $30,000 and an annual investment return of 8%, your account balance after 30 years would be over $2,000,000! All from *tax-deductible* employer contributions of only $900,000.

In short, qualified plans offer you the opportunity to tailor an employee retirement program to meet your needs as well as your employees'. We've discussed only a few of the advantages and considerations for you to study in this book. There are certainly many others. Any of these plans can be very successful with sound design, promotion, administration, and implementation. Choosing the plan that's best for your organization requires a thorough analysis of the following factors:

### *Workforce Demographics*

Who comprises your workforce? Are they predominantly younger or older? Are they mostly primary or secondary wage earners? Is your workforce primarily married or single? How high is your employee turnover? Is it easy for you to replace good workers? Are your employees highly motivated and productive?

### *Cost Considerations*

How much money do you desire to spend on deferred compensation and retirement benefits? Consider both the funding and the administration of the plans.

Do you expect your budget for these programs to rise, stay the same, or decrease in the future? How much do you feel employees should contribute toward their own retirement?

| Costs and Benefits of Different Plans | | | | |
|---|---|---|---|---|
| Type of Plan | Maximum Contribution | Required Contribution? | Who Benefits? | Administrative Costs |
| Defined Benefit | $70,000+ | Yes | Older | High |
| Profit Sharing | $30,000 | No | Younger | Moderate |
| Money Purchase | $30,000 | Yes | Younger | Moderate |
| Age-Weighted | $30,000 | No | Older | Moderate + |
| 401(k) | $ 9,500 | No | Younger | High |
| SEP | $30,000 | No | Younger | None |

## *Administrative Requirements*

Do you have staff people capable of administering the plans efficiently? Are there reliable resources available outside your company to provide these services efficiently, accurately, and economically?

## *Legislative/Tax Regulations*

How does current and pending legislation affect your current plans? Which plans make the most sense for your organization based on legislative requirements and tax guidelines?

## *Employee Expectations*

What do your employees expect in the way of retirement plan benefits? Have they indicated the plan features they prefer through surveys, exit interviews, or the "grapevine"?

## *Other Considerations*

Are you actively seeking ways to attract additional capital funding for your company? Are your owners or other key personnel involved in estate planning decisions?

The answers to these questions will dictate which types of qualified plans are best for you.

# APPENDIX

# Appendix A

## *The Omnibus Budget Reconciliation Act of 1993*

T he Omnibus Budget Reconciliation Act of 1993 (OBRA '93) passed both the House (with a two vote majority) and the Senate (with Vice President Gore casting the tie-breaking vote) and was signed into law by President Clinton on August 10, 1993. Following is a brief summary of the provisions which affected retirement plans and how those changes have affected contribution calculations each year since OBRA was enacted.

### *Reduction in the Amount of Compensation for SEPs and QPs*

#### *Prior Law:*
The amount of a participant's compensation that could be taken into account under a SEP or qualified plan was limited to $200,000 indexed for cost of living adjustments. For 1993 the $200,000 was increased to $235,840. This compensation limit is used to determine the maximum amount an employer may deduct as well as to determine the amount of a contribution under the plan or on behalf of a participant.

#### *OBRA '93:*
In general, effective for plan years beginning after December 31, 1993, the amount of a participant's compensation which may be taken into account for determining plan contributions for participants and employer deductions has been **reduced** to **$150,000**.

This amount is also indexed for cost of living adjustments, however, the indexing will be made only in increments of $10,000. Therefore, if the cost of living adjustment is less than $10,000 for a given year, there will be no increase in the dollar limitation for such year. As of 1996, that dollar limitation remained at $150,000. We are finally seeing an increase to $160,000 in 1997.

This reduction in the compensation limit to $150,000 has affected SEPs, qualified plans [money purchase, profit-sharing including 401(k), and defined benefit plans], §403(b) plans, and Salary Reduction SEPs.

| | Prior Limitations | Current Limitations |
|---|---|---|
| **SEP Plan** | 15% times $235,840 = $35,376 which must be capped at **$30,000** | 15% times $160,000 = **$24,000** |
| **Profit-Sharing** | 15% times $235,840 = $35,376 which must be capped at **$30,000** | 15% times $160,000 = **$24,000** |
| **Money Purchase** | 25% times $235,840 = $58,960 which must be capped at **$30,000** | 25% times $160,000 = $40,000 which must be capped at **$30,000** |
| **Combined Profit Sharing** *or* **SEP Plan** *and* **Money Purchase** | 25% (total between both plans) times $235,840 = $58,960 which must be capped at **$30,000** | 25% (total between both plans) times $160,000 = $40,000 which must be capped at **$30,000** |

**Note that under a SEP or Profit Sharing Plan alone, a $30,000 contribution cannot be reached in 1997. The maximum contribution is effectively reduced to $24,000!**

# Appendix B

## *Unrelated Business Taxable Income*

One of the many benefits derived from having a qualified retirement plan is that income from the plan investments is generally not taxed until distribution. However, if an individual owns an asset in his retirement plan which generates *Unrelated Business Taxable Income (UBTI),* the plan may be subject to taxation. Assets which tend to generate UBTI are certain limited partnerships and limited liability companies. Stocks (excluding publicly traded limited partnerships), bonds, and mutual funds generally do not generate UBTI, unless they are purchased through a "debt-financed" arrangement.

### *IRAs & SEPs*

Generally, IRAs and SEPs that receive $1,000 or more of gross UBTI during a single tax year must file IRS Form 990-T with the IRS on or before the April 15 tax-filing deadline, and all applicable taxes are to be paid from trust assets. Plans that receive less than $1,000 of gross unrelated business taxable income are currently not required to file.

### *Business Retirement Plans*

If the combined assets of all participants in a business retirement plan [such as a profit-sharing plan, a money purchase pension plan, or a 401(k) plan] generate $1,000 or more of gross UBTI during a single tax year, then the plan must file Form 990-T with the IRS on or before the plan's tax filing deadline. All applicable taxes are to be paid from trust assets. If the amount of gross UBTI is less than $1,000, then the plan is not required to file.

Participants in IRA, SEP, and other qualified retirement plans should be aware that UBTI losses may offset future UBTI income, so it may be beneficial to file even in years where UBTI losses negate the filing requirement.

Information concerning UBTI is generally reported on a Schedule K-1, which is prepared by the investment sponsor. The investment sponsors usually begin mailing Schedule K-1s sometime in February or March.

Any income or loss reflected on a Schedule K-1 for a retirement plan should not be combined and/or reported on an individual's personal tax return. The K-1 should reflect the trust's tax identification number and not the individual participant's tax identification number or Social Security number.

# Appendix C

## *Selecting a Beneficiary*

R etirement plan benefits are often the largest asset in a participant's estate. Choosing a beneficiary is a vital part of the participant's estate plan. This section reviews the considerations behind this important choice from the perspective of the retirement plan participant. A plan participant is often best advised to designate his spouse as beneficiary. Designation of the spouse offers the following advantages:

***Rollover to IRA.*** If a retirement plan participant dies and the spouse receives a distribution that would qualify for tax-free rollover to an individual retirement account (IRA) if paid to the participant, the spouse may roll the distribution over to the spouse's own IRA. Distributions to beneficiaries other than the surviving spouse cannot be rolled over.

***Maximum deferral of commencement of distributions.*** If a retirement plan participant dies before benefits have begun to be distributed and the designated beneficiary is the spouse (and only the spouse), then the surviving spouse may elect to defer the commencement of minimum distributions under Code Section 401(a)(9) over the spouse's life or life expectancy until the December 31 of the year in which the participant would have attained age 70½. If the designated beneficiary were not the spouse, then the distributions over the designated beneficiary's life or life expectancy would have to begin by December 31 of the year following the year in which the participant dies. If no designated beneficiary exists, or if distributions are not to be made over the designated beneficiary's life or life expectancy, then the participant's entire interest in the plan must be distributed within five years after the participant's death.

***Deferral of excess retirement accumulation tax.*** If the participant's retirement plan benefits are so large that the estate would be subject to the 15 percent excise tax on excess retirement accumulations, and if the spouse is the beneficiary of all of the benefits (except for de minimus benefits), the spouse may elect to treat the benefits as belonging to the spouse for purposes of that tax. Such an election avoids payment of the excise tax upon the death of the participant. No other beneficiary can make such an election.

### WHEN A TRUST DESIGNATION MAY BE BETTER

Despite the advantages of designating the spouse as beneficiary, a retirement plan participant may want to designate a trust as a beneficiary in the following circumstances:

***Maximize shelter of assets under "unified credit."*** The participant may have established a "credit shelter trust" to take advantage of the $600,000 that, by means of the participant's lifetime unified credit," can be transferred free of federal estate tax upon the participant's death. If the participant needs to fund such a trust with retirement plan assets (due to a lack of other sufficient or appropriate assets in the estate), the trust could be designated as beneficiary.

***Protect assets from spouse's mismanagement.*** The participant's spouse may be an inappropriate person to manage the retirement plan assets. If so, the participant may want to have the assets paid to a trust for the benefit of the spouse. If the spouse is the sole beneficiary of the trust income and principal, the retirement plan benefits qualify for the marital deduction and thus avoid federal estate tax upon the participant's death.

***Control ultimate disposition of plan assets.*** If the spouse is the beneficiary but does not use all of the retirement plan assets before death, the disposition of the balance of the assets will be determined by the spouse (by will or by beneficiary designation). However, the participant may not want the spouse to be able to control the ultimate disposition of the asset balance, particularly if the participant has children from a prior marriage or other desired beneficiaries. In such case, the participant may want to designate as beneficiary a "qualified terminable interest property" (QTIP) trust that qualifies for the marital deduction. A QTIP trust is designed to have, as ultimate beneficiaries, individuals other than the spouse, but provides that (1) all trust income is paid to the spouse at least annually and, (2) during the life of the spouse, trust principal cannot be paid to anyone other than the spouse.

## DEFERRING DISTRIBUTIONS WITH A TRUST AS BENEFICIARY

For purposes of the minimum distribution rules of Code Section 401(a)(9), a "designated beneficiary" is defined by statute as any individual designated as beneficiary by the participant. Thus, the general rule is that, if a participant names a trust as beneficiary, the retirement plan benefits must be distributed under the more rapid schedule that applies when the participant dies without a "designated beneficiary." [If the participant dies without a "designated beneficiary" before distributions have begun, the participant's entire interest in the plan must be distributed within five years after the participant's death. If the participant dies without a "designated beneficiary" after distributions have begun, the distributions must be made over the participant's life or remaining life expectancy. However, the IRS has determined by regulation that, when a trust is named as plan beneficiary, the trust beneficiaries are treated as plan beneficiaries and the required distribution period can thus be measured by the life of the trust beneficiary with the shortest life expectancy, but only if the trust meets the following four requirements:

1. The trust must be valid under state law (or would be except for the fact that there is no corpus).

2. The trust beneficiaries must be identifiable from the trust document.

3. A copy of the trust document must be provided to the plan.

4. The trust must be irrevocable.

*The trust must meet these four requirements as of the later of: (1) the date on which the trust is named as beneficiary, or (2) April 1 of the year following the participant's attainment of age 70½. The trust must continue to meet the requirements at all times thereafter while the trust is named as beneficiary.*

The requirement of irrevocability is not generally a problem, because the trust need not be irrevocably named as beneficiary. However, it means that a revocable living trust (A living trust is a trust created during life, a popular estate planning tool) does not qualify. Therefore, if a revocable trust is named as beneficiary before the required beginning date for distributions at age 70½, the beneficiary should generally be changed, effective upon the required beginning date. If the age 70½ required beginning date has already occurred and distributions have begun over the joint life expectancies of the participant and an individual such as the spouse, the participant should think twice before replacing the individual beneficiary with the revocable living trust as plan beneficiary. Such replacement would require the plan distribution period to be accelerated to equal the participant's remaining life expectancy.

The most popular kind of irrevocable trust to be named as plan beneficiary is the QTIP trust, because it enables the participant to control the ultimate disposition of the plan assets after the spouse's death, as described above.

## SPOUSAL DISCLAIMERS

To permit the surviving spouse to maximize the marital deduction, a participant with a significant estate is often best advised to name a series of successive beneficiaries, with each beneficiary permitted to disclaim to the next named beneficiary. Such an arrangement allows the best beneficiary (for tax purposes and otherwise) to be chosen with the benefit of hindsight after the participant's death.

For example, the participant may designate (with the spouse's written consent) the primary beneficiary to be a credit shelter trust, the secondary beneficiary to be a marital trust or QTIP trust that qualifies for the marital deduction, and the tertiary beneficiary to be the spouse. If the retirement plan benefits were not needed to fund the credit shelter trust, its trustees could disclaim the benefits, which would then be paid to the marital or QTIP trust on an accelerated basis to qualify for the marital deduction. If, in turn, the retirement plan benefits were not needed to fund the marital or QTIP trust, the trustees of the marital or QTIP trust could disclaim the benefits, which would then be paid to the spouse. The spouse could then roll the benefits over to his own IRA or elect to defer the excess retirement accumulation tax described above.

## UNMARRIED PARTICIPANTS

A participant who is not married has relatively few planning opportunities with regard to the selection of a beneficiary. Upon the participant's death, regardless of who is named as beneficiary, the entire retirement plan interest is included in the participant's gross estate for purposes of the federal estate tax.

Unmarried plan participants often designate multiple primary beneficiaries, such as adult children, siblings, or other relatives. When multiple beneficiaries are named, the beneficiary with the shortest life expectancy is considered the "designated beneficiary" for purposes of determining the distribution period under Code Section 401(a)(9). If a trust is named as beneficiary, then the required distributions must begin over the life or life expectancy of the participant, unless the trust satisfies the four requirements mentioned above, in which case the measuring period may be the joint lives or life expectancies of the participant and the trust beneficiary with the shortest life expectancy.

SUMMARY

If retirement plan benefits constitute a significant part of the participant's estate, the participant should give careful consideration to the decision of whom to name as beneficiary. Although the spouse is generally best named as beneficiary, a carefully drafted QTIP trust is sometimes more appropriate. However, the participant can create the greatest amount of flexibility by naming a series of successive beneficiaries and planning for the use of disclaimers by the beneficiaries to achieve the best tax and estate planning results.

# Appendix D

## *Self-Employed Earned Income Calculation Worksheet*

1. Enter Net Profit from Schedule C      $____
2. Enter ½ Self-Employment Tax from Schedule SE    $____
3. Subtract Line 2 from Line 1. Enter result: (This is your Adjusted Net Profit)      $____
4. Enter *desired* plan contribution percentage: ____%
5. Enter Net Profit Equivalency percentage from chart on page 134:      ____%
6. Multiple Line 3 by Line 5. Enter result:      $____
7. Multiply Line 4 by $160,000. Enter result:      $____
8. Maximum Dollar Contribution:      $30,000
9. Enter the lesser of Lines 6, 7, or 8. (This is your plan contribution amount)      $____

*Source: Keys to Keoghs, PenServ, Inc. ©1995*

# Appendix E

## *The Small Business Job Protection Act of 1996*

President Bill Clinton signed into law the Small Business Job Protection on August 20, 1996 (P.L. 104-188). The Small Business Act, which was tied to an increase in the minimum wage, contained an array of pension simplification provisions, as well as many tax breaks for small businesses. Clinton and Republican Congressional leaders hailed the legislation as a major economic boost for small businesses and low-wage earners. "The bill makes it much easier for small businesses to offer pension plans by creating a new small business 401(k) plan," Clinton said, referring to the new SIMPLE plan. "I am very proud that the first major tax bill of this new Congress is a $21 billion tax-relief measure, not a tax increase," said House Ways and Means Committee Chairman Bill Archer (R-Tex.).

### *Highlights of the Small Business Act include:*

**Spousal IRAs.** The maximum deductible contribution to an individual retirement account (IRA) has been increased for married individuals who file a joint return where one of the spouses has no compensation. For tax years beginning after 1996, the maximum deductible amount is $2,000 for each spouse if the combined compensation of both spouses is at least equal to the contributed amount.

**New SIMPLE Retirement Plan.** Small businesses that normally employ 100 or fewer employees, paid the employees at least $5,000 in compensation in the preceding year, and do not maintain another plan may establish a Savings Incentive Match Plan for Employees (SIMPLE) for years beginning after 1996. A SIMPLE plan can be in the form of either an individual retirement account (IRA) for each employee or part of a qualified cash or deferred arrangement [401(k) plan]. Employees may make elective contributions of up to $6,000 per year to a SIMPLE plan, and employers must make matching contributions. Employees are not taxed on account assets until distributions are made, and employers generally may deduct their contributions to the plan. SIMPLE plans are not subject to the nondiscrimination rules for qualified plans, including the top-heavy rules.

**SARSEPs Repealed.** Employers are not permitted to establish salary reduction simplified employee pensions (SARSEPs) after 1996. SARSEPs established before 1997 may continue to receive contributions under the prior-law rules.

**Simplified Distribution Rules.** In order to make it easier for individuals to determine the amount of tax owed on pension and other distributions, several rules have been simplified or repealed:

- **Five-Year Averaging Repealed.** Five-year averaging for lump-sum distributions from qualified plans has been repealed for tax years beginning after 1999.

- **Exclusion for Employer-Provided Death Benefits.** The $5,000 exclusion from income for employer-provided death benefits is repealed for employees dying after the date of enactment of the Small Business Act.

- **Simplified Method for Taxing Annuity Distributions**. A simplified alternative method has been provided for determining the portion of an annuity payment from a qualified retirement plan, qualified annuity, or tax sheltered annuity that represents a nontaxable return of basis. This method, which applies an exclusion ratio equal to the annuitant's total investment in the contract as of the annuity starting date divided by the number of anticipated payments, may be used where the annuity starting date is later than the 90th day after the date of enactment of the Small Business Act.

- **Starting Date for Required Distributions**. Effective for years beginning after 1996, the requirement that all qualified plan participants who remain employed begin receiving distributions by age 70½ has been replaced with a requirement that distributions begin by April 1 of the calendar year following the later of the calendar year in which the employee reaches age 70½ or the calendar year in which the employee retires. A special rule applies to employees who are 5% owners or IRA holders, and an actuarial adjustment rule may apply to them, also.

- **Tax-Exempt Organizations Can Maintain 401(k) Plans.** For plan years beginning after 1996, The Act allows tax-exempt organizations and Indian Tribes to maintain 401(k) plans. However, state and local government plans still will not be able to maintain 401(k) arrangements (other than those grandfathered plans in existence in 1986).

# GLOSSARY
# OF
# TERMS

# GLOSSARY OF TERMS

**Accrual of Benefits**

In the case of a defined benefit pension plan, the process of accumulating pension credits for years of credited service, expressed in the form of an annual benefit to begin payment at normal retirement age. In the case of a defined contribution plan, the process of accumulating funds in the individual employee's pension account.

**Accrued Benefit**

For any retirement plan which is not a defined benefit pension plan, a participant's accrued benefit is the balance in his plan account, whether vested or not. In the case of a defined benefit pension plan, a participant's accrued benefit is his benefit as determined under the terms of the plan expressed in the form of an annual benefit commencing at normal retirement age. Under ERISA, three alternative methods of benefit accrual are allowed (see Fractional Rule; 133 1/3 Rule; 3% Method).

**Active Participant**

Individual who is a participant and for whom at any time during the taxable year benefits are accrued under the plan on his behalf, or for whom the employer is obligated to contribute to or under the plan on his behalf or for whom the employer would have been obligated to contribute to or under the plan on his behalf if any contributions were made to or under the plan.  See also Plan Participant.

## Actuarial Assumptions

Factors used by the actuary in forecasting uncertain future events affecting pension cost.  They involve such things as interest and investment earnings, mortality rates, turnover, etc.

## Actuarial Cost

A cost is characterized as actuarial if it is derived through the use of present values.  An actuarial cost is often used to associate the costs of benefits under a retirement system with the approximate time the benefits are earned.

## Actuary

A person professionally trained in the technical and mathematical aspects of insurance, pensions, and related fields. The actuary estimates how much money must be contributed to a pension fund each year in order to support the benefits that will become payable in the future.

## Ad Hoc Postretirement Adjustment

An ad hoc postretirement adjustment is one which establishes a schedule of one-time increases in retirement allowances.

## Administrator

The person designated as such by the instrument under which the plan is operated.  If the administrator is not so designated, *administrator* means the plan sponsor.  If the administrator is not designated and the plan sponsor cannot be identified, the administrator may be such person as is prescribed by regulation of the Secretary of Labor.

The administrator's responsibilities are as follows:

1. Act solely in the interest of plan participants and beneficiaries, and for the exclusive purpose of providing benefits and defraying reasonable administrative expenses.

2. Manage the plan's assets to minimize the risk of large losses.

3. Act in accordance with the documents governing the plan.

## Alienation of Benefits

ERISA provides that plan benefits cannot be assigned or alienated under a tax-qualified plan. Plan benefits cannot be paid to the employer or to a third party (except under a QDRO) when they would otherwise be paid to the participant.

## Allocation

The distribution of the employer's contribution to the account of each participant. In a profit-sharing plan, it also refers to the distribution of earnings and forfeitures for the various accounts.

## Annuity

1. A contract that provides an income for a specified period of time such as a number of years or for life.
2. The periodic payments provided under an annuity contract.
3. The specified monthly or annual payment to a pensioner. Often used synonymously with pension.

## Approved Plan

A pension, deferred profit-sharing or stock bonus plan that meets the requirements of the Internal Revenue Code and the applicable regulations. Such approval qualifies the plan for favorable tax treatment. Approval of a pension plan does not indicate any judgment regarding the plan's actuarial soundness.

## Attribution

The process of assigning pension benefits or cost to periods of employee service.

## Automatic Postretirement Adjustment

A program providing for recurring adjustments in retirement allowances on a regular basis. Contrast with Ad Hoc Postretirement Adjustment.

## Average Annual Compensation

An employee's average annual compensation is his annual compensation averaged over at least three consecutive years, under a uniform rule used for all employees. For this purpose it is acceptable to use for each employee the period of consecutive years which will produce his highest average. See also Final Average Salary.

## Beneficiary

1.  Person named by the participant in an insurance policy or pension plan to receive any benefits provided by the plan if the participant dies.

2.  A person designated by a participant, or by the terms of an employee benefit plan, who is or may become entitled to a benefit thereunder.

## Benefit

Rights of the participant to either cash or services after meeting the eligibility requirements of the pension or other benefit plans. Pension benefits usually refer to monthly payments payable on retirement or disability.

## Beta

Beta (market sensitivity) is a measure of extent to which a fund's portfolio fluctuates with the market as represented by the S&P 500. To calculate beta, you measure the sensitivity of the fund's portfolio to market patterns. Beta is a statistical estimate of the average change in a fund's rate of return corresponding to a 1% change in the market.

## Break in Service

Under ERISA, a calendar year, plan year, or other 12 consecutive month period designated by the plan during which a plan participant does not complete more than 500 hours of services.

## Certificate of Deposit (CD)

A written certification by a bank or a savings and loan association that a fixed dollar amount has been deposited with it for a fixed period of time at a predetermined rate of interest. Certificates are registered in the name of the depositor and are issued in negotiable and non-negotiable form. If the depositor needs the money before the expressed maturity, a negotiable certificate frequently can be sold to certain money brokers at the then-existing money rate.

## Certified Employee Benefit Specialist (CEBS)

A designation granted jointly by the International Foundation of Employee Benefit Plans and the Wharton School of the University of Pennsylvania to individuals who complete ten college level courses and examinations in the areas of design and operation of employee benefit plans and who pledge to a code of ethical standards and continuing education.

## Certified Pension Consultant (CPC)

A designation awarded by the American Society of Pension Actuaries. Holders must combine required experience with passing three examinations covering employee benefits fundamentals.

## Certified Public Accountant

A professional license granted by the various states to persons meeting certain educational, experience and examination requirements. These requirements vary from state to state, but typically they include a college degree with accounting and auditing course-work and qualifying experience. The examinations include passing the Uniform CPA Examination, covering accounting theory and practice, auditing, and business law.

## Chartered Financial Analyst (CFA)

Awarded by the Institute of Chartered Financial Analysts. Holders must combine required experience and education with passing three examinations covering ethical and professional standards, securities laws and regulations, financial accounting, etc.

## Chartered Financial Consultant (CFC)

A designation granted by the American College to individuals who complete a ten course program in the areas of personal financial and retirement planning and who pledge to a code of ethical standards and continuing education.

## Chartered Life Underwriter (CLU)

A designation granted by the American College to individuals who complete a ten course program in the areas of insurance and estate planning and who pledge to a code of ethical standards and continuing education.

## Cliff Vesting

Full (100%) vesting after $x$ years of service. All benefits vested after $x$ years.

## Commingled Funds

The collective investment of the assets of a number of small pension funds, usually through a bank-administered plan allowing for broader and more efficient investing.

## Compounding

The arithmetic process of finding the final value of an investment or series of investments when compound interest is applied. That is, interest is earned on the interest as well as on the initial principal.

## Constructive Receipt

Income, although not actually transferred to a taxpayer's possession, is constructively received by him in the taxable year during which it is credited to the taxpayer's account, or set apart for him, so he may draw upon it at any time.

## Contribution Limits

The maximum dollar limit on annual additions (employer contributions, certain employee contributions and forfeitures) for an employee under defined contribution plans of an employer.

## Corporation

An artificial being composed of one or more individuals and established by law for some specific purpose or purposes whose existence, power, and scope of action are determined by its charter.

## Cost/Benefit Analysis

A comparison of the cost of an action with the economic benefits it produces through elimination of other direct and indirect costs.

## Cost-of-Living Allowance or Adjustment (COLA)

An increase (or decrease) in wages or pension benefits according to the rise (or fall) in the cost of living as measured by some index, often the Consumer Price Index (CPI).

## Deferred Compensation

Arrangements by which compensation to employees for past or current services is postponed until some future date. Pension and profit-sharing plans are tax-favored (qualified) deferred compensation plans.

## Deferred Compensation Plan

Any plan where employees can accumulate money on a tax-deferred basis. A qualified plan can have the option of permitting employees to withdraw assets without penalty for certain "emergency" situations specified in the plan. Many also give employees the option of taking the benefit in cash. A deferred compensation plan can be combined with other plans such as profit-sharing plans.

## Defined Benefit Plan

Both ERISA and the Internal Revenue Code define a *defined benefit plan* as any plan that is not an individual account plan. Under a defined benefit plan, there is a definite formula by which the employee's benefits will be measured. This formula may provide that benefits be a particular percentage of the employee's average compensation over his entire service or over a particular number of years; it may provide for a flat monthly payment or it may provide a definite amount for each year of service, expressed either as a percentage of his compensation for each year of service or as a flat dollar amount for each year of service. In plans of this type, the employer's contributions are determined actuarially. No individual accounts are maintained as is done in defined contribution plans. (Defined benefit plans are subject to regulation by the PBGC and are "pension plans" under the Internal Revenue Code. That is, they are designed primarily for retirement.)

## Defined Contribution Plan

A *defined contribution* or *individual account plan* is defined by the Internal Revenue Code and ERISA as a plan which provides for an individual account for each participant and for benefits based solely on (1) the amount contributed to the participant's account plus (2) any income, expenses, gains and losses, and forfeitures of accounts of other participants which may be allocated to the participant's account.

## Discretionary Formula

A profit-sharing or SEP plan contribution arrangement that enables the employer to determine or change annually the amount or the formula for its plan contribution.

## Disqualified Person

The IRC term roughly equivalent to "party in interest." The term *disqualified person* also includes a highly compensated employee; this is a person earning 10% or more of the wages paid by (1) an employer, any of whose employees are covered by the plan; (2) an employee organization, any of whose members are covered by the plan; (3) a 50% or more owner of an employer or employee organization; (4) a corporation, partnership, trust or estate 50% or more owned by a fiduciary, a person providing services to the plan, or a person described in (1)-(3) above.

## Dividend

The proportion of net earnings paid to its stockholders by a corporation.

## Dollar Cost Averaging

A policy by which the same dollar amount is placed in one or more common stocks at fixed successive intervals, thereby enabling the investor to average the purchase of his shares over a period of time. Assuming that each investment is of the same number of dollars, a greater number of shares are purchased when the price is low and fewer shares are purchased when the price is high. Thus a satisfactory average price is obtained which precludes the investor from buying all the shares at the high levels of the market.

## Double-Dipping

The term has been variously applied to mean:

1. Qualifying for, and obtaining, pension benefits under two or more plans;
2. Qualifying for, and obtaining, pension benefits under one plan while remaining employed by another employer;
3. Qualifying for, and obtaining, Social Security retirement benefits while also qualifying for and obtaining retirement benefits under a civil service retirement system, particularly a federal plan.

## Double Taxation

"Double taxation of dividends." The federal government taxes corporate profits once as corporate income; any part of the remaining profits distributed as dividends to stockholders may be taxed again as income to the recipient stockholders.

## Earned Income

Under federal income tax laws, the income of an individual from services actually rendered. Thus excluding, for example, income from the sale or rental of property, interest income, etc.

## Elapsed Time Method of Counting Service

A method for determining a worker's time in service by subtracting the hire-in date from the termination date.

## Eligibility Requirements

Conditions that an employee must satisfy to participate in a plan; or conditions that an employee must satisfy to obtain a benefit.

## Eligible Employees

Those members of a group who have met the eligibility requirements under a pension or other retirement plan.

## Employee Benefit Plan

A plan established or maintained by an employer or employee organization, or both. The purpose is to provide employees with a certain benefit such as pension, profit-sharing, stock bonus, thrift, medical, sickness, accident, or disability benefits.

## Employee Retirement Income Security Act of 1974 (ERISA)

This requires that persons engaged in the administration, supervision, and management of pension monies have a fiduciary responsibility to ensure that all investment-related decisions are made (1) with the care, skill, prudence and diligence... that a prudent man...familiar with such matters would use...and (2) by diversifying the investments...so as to minimize risk. This wording mandates two significant changes in traditional investment practice: (1) the age-old "prudent man" rule has been replaced by the notion of a prudent "expert"; (2) the notion of a prudent investment has been replaced by the concept of a prudent portfolio.

ERISA also established an insurance program designed to guarantee workers receipt of pension benefits if their pension plan should terminate. It regulates the majority of private pension and welfare group benefit plans in the U.S.

## Employee Stock Ownership Plan (ESOP)

An employee stock ownership plan is a qualified stock bonus plan or a qualified stock bonus and money purchase plan. Like a stock bonus plan, the contributions need not be dependent on profits and benefits are distributable in the stock of the employer corporation. Often the employee stock ownership plan is used as a financing vehicle for the employer corporation: The plan borrows money with which to purchase employer stock and the borrowed money is paid to the employer for its stock. The loan is repaid with annual employer contributions. See also Payroll Stock Ownership Plan.

## Excess Contribution

If the employer contributes more than the maximum amount deductible under the minimum funding rules, the excess will not be currently deductible. However, the excess may be carried over to another year or years and deducted at that time (within the maximum deduction limits).

## Fair Market Value (FMV)

The value of property established between a willing buyer and a willing seller in an arm's length transaction.

## Fiduciary

Indicates the relationship of trust and confidence where one person (the fiduciary) holds or controls property for the benefit of another person. For example, the relationship between a trustee and the beneficiaries of the trust.

Under ERISA (the Employee Retirement Income Security Act of 1974), any person who (a) exercises any discretionary authority or control over the management of a plan or the management or disposition of its assets, (b) renders investment advice for a fee with respect to the funds or property of a plan, or has the authority to do so, or (c) has any discretionary authority or responsibility in the administration of a plan.

One who acts in a capacity of trust and who is therefore accountable for whatever actions may be construed by the courts as breaching that trust. Under ERISA, fiduciaries must discharge their duties solely in the interest of the participants and beneficiaries of an employee benefit plan. In addition, a fiduciary must act exclusively for the purpose of providing benefits to participants and beneficiaries in defraying reasonable expenses of the plan. See also Prudent Man Rule.

**Final Average Salary**

That measure of a participant's level of earnings which is based on his average rate of salary for a specified period of time, usually the three, five, or ten years immediately preceding retirement. A participant's final average salary may be one of the factors used in determining the amount of his benefits.

**Forfeitures**

Amounts contributed on behalf of terminated, nonvested participants. In a pension plan, such amounts must be applied to reducing future employer contributions. In a profit-sharing plan, such amounts may be allocated to the accounts of remaining participants.

**401(k) Plan**

A defined contribution plan established by an employer which enables employees to make pretax contributions by salary reduction agreements structured within the format of a cash or deferred plan.

## 403(b) Plan

A defined contribution plan available to certain tax exempt organizations and public schools for their employees.

## Graded Vesting

A vesting schedule that calls for partial vesting after a specific length of service. The vested portion is increased each year until it reaches 100%.

## Gross Income

The total amount of money received from income property or a business, before operating expenses, taxes, depreciation, commissions, salaries, fees, etc. are deducted.

## Hour of Service

As used in connection with minimum participation standards, a time of service determined under regulations prescribed by the Secretary of Labor.

**HR-10 Plan -** See Keogh Plan.

## Immediate Vesting

That form of vesting under which rights to vested benefits are acquired by a participant, commencing immediately upon his entry into the plan.

## Income and Service Benefit Formula

A retirement benefit formula based on income and credited service, such as 1% of average annual income multiplied by the years of service.

### Income-Based Benefit Formula

A retirement formula based solely on income such as 50% of the final yearly salary.

### Individual Retirement Account (IRA)

A retirement savings program for individuals to which yearly (often tax deductible) contributions up to a specified limit can be made. The amounts contributed are not taxed until withdrawn. Withdrawal is not permitted, without penalty, until the individual reaches age 59½. See also Individual Retirement Plans.

### Individual Retirement Plans

Effective for tax years beginning after December 31, 1981, employees and self-employed persons receiving compensation can establish their own individual retirement plans, even if they are already covered under tax-qualified plans (including HR-10 or Keogh plans), government plans, or certain annuities.

### Integration Level

The compensation level below which, under a plan's benefit formula, compensation is excluded in the computation of benefits or contributions.

### Integration With Social Security

A plan wherein the benefits are integrated with the Social Security benefit. Under regular corporate plans, the regulations define the percentages applicable to the various benefits. Under a self-employed program, the only offset permissible is the amount of the Social Security tax paid for the employee. If more than one plan is instituted for the same company, only one program may be integrated.

The basic concept of integration is that the benefits of the employer's plan must be linked with Social Security benefits in such a manner that employees earning more than the taxable wage base will not receive combined benefits under the two programs which are proportionately greater than the benefits for employees earning less than the taxable wage base.

**Internal Revenue Code (IRC)**

As amended, this code is the basic federal tax law.

**Internal Revenue Service (IRS)**

A government agency charged with the collection of taxes. The income tax code and regulations often affect the procedures and methods of accounting.

**Investment Policy**

A term commonly used to describe how contributions to an employee benefit plan are utilized from the time they are received until benefits are paid. Under ERISA, a written investment policy is required.

**Investment Policy Statement**

The statement of policy is the communication of a risk policy to the fund's investment manager(s). It states unambiguously the degree of investment risk that fiduciaries are willing to undertake with pension trust assets. A statement of investment policy differs importantly from a statement of investment objectives. An investment policy prescribes acceptable course of action; a policy can be acted upon, implemented. An investment objective (such as a performance standard) is a desired result. A manager cannot implement an objective; he can only pursue a course of action, consistent with investment policy, which he believes offers a reasonable likelihood of realizing the objective. Therefore, in drafting instructions for an investment manager, primary emphasis should be on stating the investment, or risk, policy clearly.

**IRA** - See Individual Retirement Account.

## Joint and Survivor Annuity

A contract that provides income periodically, payable during the longer life-time of two persons. The amount payable may decrease when one or the other dies. The contingent annuitant is usually the spouse.

## Keogh Plan

A retirement plan for self-employed persons and their employees to which yearly tax deductible contributions up to a specified limit can be made, if the plan meets certain requirements of the Internal Revenue Code. Keogh plans, also known as HR-10 plans, include defined benefit and money purchase plans as well as profit-sharing plans.

## Key Employee

A participant who, at any time during the plan year or any of the four preceding years, is (or was): (1) an officer, (2) one of the ten employees owning the largest interest in the employer, (3) a more than 5% owner of the employer or (4) a more than 1% owner earning more than $150,000.

## Letter Ruling

A private ruling issued by the IRS in response to a request from a taxpayer about the tax consequences of a proposed or completed transaction. Private Letter Rulings are published informally by several publishers. They are not considered to be precedents for use by taxpayers other than the one who requested the ruling, but they do give an indication of the current attitude of the IRS toward a particular type of transaction.

## Master Plan

A defined benefit or defined contribution plan that has been prepared by a sponsoring organization which provides for a single trust account in which all adopting employers must invest their plan contributions; the sponsoring organization must have the plan approved by the Internal Revenue Service.

## Minimum Funding

The minimum amount that must be contributed by an employer who has a defined benefit, money purchase, or target benefit pension plan. If the employer fails to meet these minimum standards, in the absence of a waiver from the IRS, an excise tax will be imposed on the amount of the deficiency.

## Mistake of Fact

Ignorance or forgetfulness of a fact which is material to the creation of a legal obligation.

## Money Purchase Pension Plan

A type of pension plan in which the employer's contributions are determined for, and allocated with respect to, specific individuals, usually as a percentage of compensation. The benefits for each employee are the amounts which can be provided by the sums contributed to him.

A money purchase pension plan is an individual account plan, as defined in Section 3(34) of ERISA, other than a profit-sharing plan or a stock bonus plan, in which the employer's contributions are fixed or determinable.

## One Year Break In Service

As used in connection with the minimum vesting standards, a calendar year, plan year, or other 12 consecutive month period designated by the plan during which the participant has not completed more than 500 hours of service.

## Owner-Employee

Self-employed individual who owns the entire interest in an unincorporated business, or a partner who owns more than 10% of the capital or profit interest of the partnership.

## Participation Requirements

Most pension and other employee benefit plans provide that a new employee must wait a specified length of time before he is eligible to participate in the plan. Generally, ERISA sets the maximum waiting period at one year.

Some plans provide for 100% vesting of an employee's accrued benefits immediately upon commencing participation. ERISA permits these plans to require an employee to complete a maximum of three years of service before commencing to participate.

## Past Service

The years of service rendered by the employee to the employer, prior to the inception of the plan or prior to the employee's entry into the program.

## Payroll Stock Ownership Plan (PAYSOP)

An ESOP eligible for tax credits based on employee payroll; replaced TRASOPs in 1983. A PAYSOP must meet special tax credit ESOP requirements, and not more than one-third of the corporation's contributions for a year can be allocated to officers, shareholders owning more than 10% of the employer's stock (other than stock held under the plan) or employees whose compensation exceeds twice the dollar limits on contributions. See also *Employee Stock Ownership Plan (ESOP)* and *Tax Reduction Act of 1975.*

## Pension

A series of periodic payments, usually for life, payable monthly or at other specified intervals. The term is frequently used to describe the part of a retirement allowance financed by employer contributions.

A regular payment, usually monthly, to a person who has retired from employment because of advanced age or disability.

## Pension Benefit Formula

The basis for determining payments to which participants may be entitled under a pension plan. Pension benefit formulas usually refer to the employee's service or compensation or both.

## Pension Benefit Guaranty Corporation (PBGC)

The federal agency, established as a nonprofit corporation, charged with administering the plan termination provisions of ERISA Title IV and the Multiemployer Pension Plan Amendments Act of 1980.

## Pension Plan

A plan that provides benefits, after retirement, from a trust or other separately maintained fund. The amount of benefits is either specified or can be calculated in accordance with a set formula based on various factors such as age, earnings and service, but not profits. The amount of annual contributions needed to provide the specified benefits can be estimated actuarially and does not depend upon profits.

## Plan Document

The plan document is often separate from the trust agreement in order to allow plan modifications without frequent trust agreement amendments.

## Plan Participant

Any employee or former employee of an employer, or any member or former member of an employee organization, who is or may become eligible to receive a benefit of any type from an employee benefit plan, or whose beneficiaries may be eligible to receive any such benefits. See also *Participation Requirements*.

## Plan Sponsor

(a) The employer, in the case of an employee benefit plan maintained by a single employer; (b) the employee organization, in the case of a plan maintained by an employee organization; (c) the association, committee, joint board of trustees, or other similar group of representatives of the parties involved, in the case of a plan maintained by one or more employers and one or more employee organizations.

## Plan Termination

ERISA requires that all accrued benefits (to the extent funded) must be fully vested upon the termination or partial termination of a plan. (A partial termination might result from a large reduction of the workforce or a sizable reduction of benefits under the plan.)

## Plan Year

The calendar, policy or fiscal year on which the records of the plan are kept.

## Pooled Trust

A common trust fund generally sponsored by one employer and used to accumulate the assets of different plans of the employer and its subsidiaries.

## Profit-Sharing Plan

Plan established and maintained by an employer to provide for the participation in the company's profits by the employees or their beneficiaries. The plan must provide a definite predetermined formula for allocating the contributions made to the plan among the participants and for distributing the fund accumulated under the plan after a fixed number of years, the attainment of a stated age, or upon the prior occurrence of some event such as disability, retirement, death, or termination of employment. Deferred profit-sharing plans are subject to the participation, vesting, reporting and disclosure, and fiduciary rules of ERISA. They are excluded from the funding and plan termination provisions of the act.

*Current profit-sharing plan (cash).* Profits paid directly to employees in cash, check or stock as soon as profits are determined.

*Deferred profit-sharing plan.* A qualified program of retirement benefits wherein the employer provides retirement benefits subject to a written agreement and based on the limitations described in the Internal Revenue Code. The employee's benefits at retirement are based strictly upon the sum total of the contributions made and the investment result thereon.

**Prohibited Transactions**

With certain exceptions, a trustee or other plan fiduciary may not engage in any financial transaction with the employer or individuals in control of the employer (referred to as "parties-in-interest" under the regulatory provisions and as "disqualified persons" under the tax provisions) if he knows or should have known that such transaction is prohibited by ERISA. This includes the selling or leasing of property, the lending of money, the furnishing of goods, services or facilities, or the transfer of any assets to or for the use of a party in interest (or disqualified person). In addition, plans other than eligible individual account plans may not invest more than 10% of plan assets in the employer's securities and/or real property. A plan may not hold or acquire an employer security or employer real property that is not a "qualifying employer security" or "qualifying employer real property."

**Prototype Plan**

A standardized plan, approved and qualified as to its content by Internal Revenue Service, which is made available by investment brokerage firms, insurance companies, banks, and mutual funds for the use of employers. See also *Master Plan.*

**Prudent Man Rule**

A common-law standard applicable to the investment of trust funds. Briefly stated:

All that can be required of a trustee in the investment of trust funds is that he conduct himself faithfully and exercise sound discretion. He is to observe how men of prudence, discretion and intelligence manage their own affairs, not in regard to speculation, but in regard to the permanent disposition of their funds, considering the probable income as well as the probable safety of the capital to be invested.

Under ERISA:     ...a fiduciary shall discharge his duties... with the care, skill, prudence and diligence under the circumstances then prevailing that a prudent man acting in a like capacity and familiar with such matters would use in the conduct of an enterprise of a like character and with like aims.

An investment standard adapted by the majority of states that allows a fiduciary to invest in only those securities which would be acquired by prudent men of discretion and intelligence who are seeking a reasonable return and preservation of their capital. Some states have a legal list published by the Superintendent of Banking to which savings banks, trust funds, and similar institutions must adhere.

## Qualified Domestic Relations Order (QDRO)

A domestic relations order is a judgment, decree or order (including approval of property settlement agreement) that (1) relates to the provision of child support, alimony payments or marital property rights to a spouse, former spouse, child or other dependent of a participant and (2) is made pursuant to a state domestic relations law (including a community property law). A domestic relations order is a qualified domestic relations order if it creates or recognizes the existence of an alternate payee's right to, or assigns to an alternate payee the right to, receive all or a portion of the benefits payable to a participant under a plan, specifies required information and does not alter the amount or form of plan benefits. An alternate payee is a spouse, former spouse, child or other dependent of a participant who is recognized by domestic relations order as having a right to receive all, or a portion of, the benefits under a plan with respect to the participant.

### Qualified Plan

A plan that the Internal Revenue Service approves as meeting the requirements of Section 401(a) of the Internal Revenue Code. Such plans receive tax advantages.

### Revenue Procedure

Issued by the IRS, it is somewhat similar to a Revenue Ruling but deals with procedural matters or details the requirements to be followed in connection with various dealings with the IRS. Revenue procedures also set forth guidelines that the IRS follows in handling certain tax matters.

### Revenue Ruling

Issued by the IRS, these rulings express the views of the IRS about the tax results that apply to a specific problem.

### Rollover

In order to provide greater investment flexibility, an individual is permitted to shift his investment in one individual retirement plan to another without incurring any tax liability. These shifts are referred to as "rollovers" and constructive receipt of plan assets by the plan participant or beneficiary.

Tax-free rollovers are permitted for the movement of amounts from a tax-qualified plan to an individual retirement plan or to another tax-qualified plan. The amounts, frequency and timing of tax-free rollovers are restricted under the regulations.

### Rule of 72

A convenient technique for either mental or pencil and paper estimation of compound interest rates, derived from the fact that a 7.2% return per year is the interest rate that will double the value of an investment in ten years. Hence, "years to double" an investment with a given annual rate of return can be estimated by dividing the rate of return into 72.

**Self-Employed Retirement Plan** - See Keogh Plan

**Social Security Integration** - See Integration With Social Security.

**Stock Bonus Plan**

A plan established and maintained by an employer to provide benefits similar to those of a profit-sharing plan. The contributions by the employer are not necessarily dependent upon profits and the benefits are distributable in stock of the employer company. For the purpose of allocating and distributing the stock of the employer which is to be shared among employees or their beneficiaries, such a plan is subject to the same requirements as a profit-sharing plan.

**Stock Purchase Plan**

A deferred profit-sharing plan which provides that an employee's share of the fund may be invested at his option in the employer's securities.

**Subchapter S Corporation**

An election available to a corporation to be treated as a partnership for income tax purposes. To be eligible to make the election, a corporation must meet certain requirements as to kind and number of shareholders, classes of stock, and sources of income.

**Summary Plan Description (SPD)**

A requirement of ERISA for a written statement of a plan in an easy-to-read form, including a statement of eligibility, coverage, employee rights, and appeal procedure.

**Target Benefit Plan**

A defined contribution plan for which contributions are based upon an actuarial valuation designed to provide a target benefit to each participant upon retirement. The plan does not guarantee that such benefit will be paid. Its only obligation is to pay whatever benefit can be provided by the amount in the participant's account. It is a variation of the money purchase pension plan.

**Tax Equity and Fiscal Responsibility Act of 1982 (TEFRA)**

Lowered limits on contributions and benefits for corporate plans; certain loans from the plan to be treated as distributions; reduced estate tax exclusion for retirement plan death benefits; repealed special Keogh plan and Subchapter S restrictions; added "top-heavy" plan requirements.

**Tax Reduction Act of 1975**

Provided special investment credit incentives for establishment of ESOPs (originally known as TRASOPs and changed to tax credit ESOPs by the Technical Corrections Act of 1979). The Tax Reform Act of 1976 extended these credits and further modified the applicable rules.

**Taxable Wage Base**

"Taxable wage base" means, with respect to any year, the maximum amount of earnings which may be considered wages for such year under the Internal Revenue Code; i.e., Social Security wage base.

## Thrift Plan

A defined contribution plan to which employees make contributions. Incentive matching or partially matching contributions are also made on behalf of the participating employees by the employer.

## Top-Heavy Plan

Beginning in 1984, a plan that primarily benefits key employees is considered "top-heavy" and qualifies for favorable tax treatment only if, in addition to the regular qualification requirements, it meets several special requirements.

**TRASOP** - See Tax Reduction Act of 1975.

## Vesting

An employee's right to receive a present or future pension benefit vests when it is no longer contingent upon his remaining in the service of the employer. Employee contributions are always fully vested. However, earnings upon such contributions may not be vested or may be paid at a specified rate, depending upon plan provisions. A vested benefit may be paid as a lump sum or, frequently, is paid as a deferred annuity upon retirement. See also *Vesting Schedules.*

## Vesting Schedules

The Tax Reform Act of 1986 made vesting more rapid, with two new minimum schedules: 100% vesting after five years of service; and graduated vesting beginning after three years, with 100% vesting after seven years. Class year vesting is no longer permitted. If a plan has immediate 100% vesting, the eligibility period may be extended to two years of service.

# TOPICAL INDEX

235

# About the Author

D. Kirk Buchanan is Vice President of Retirement Services at IFG Asset Management Services, Inc., the integrated product management arm within Inter-Regional Financial Group, Inc. (IFG). IFG is the parent company of Dain Bosworth Incorporated and Rauscher Pierce Refsnes, Inc., two premier  regional investment banking and brokerage firms. With an extensive background in the brokerage industry, Kirk has focused his expertise on pension and retirement plan administration and marketing since 1985.

He obtained his bachelor's degree in Business and Professional Development from Amber University in Dallas. He has also attended Southern Methodist University (SMU) in Dallas for postgraduate studies. In addition, he holds a Certificate in Pension Law and Administration from The Philadelphia Institute.

Kirk has lectured on retirement plans across the nation and is recognized for his two previous books, *Understanding IRAs* (1990) and *The IRA Explanation* (1994,1996,1997). In addition, he has written for various news publications and trade journals.

He is an active member of the International Foundation of Employee Benefit Plans, a non-profit organization dedicated exclusively to the exchange of information and education for those who serve employee benefit plans. He is also a member of the American Compensation Association, as well as The Profit Sharing Council of America.

# NOTES

# NOTES

# NOTES

# NOTES

# NOTES

# NOTES

# NOTES

# NOTES

# NOTES